20 Stocks Under $20 with 10x Growth Potential

The Best Low-Priced Stocks Poised for Massive Growth

By William C. Ledger

Financial Disclaimer

The information in this book is provided for educational and informational purposes only and does not constitute financial, investment, or trading advice. The author is not a licensed financial advisor. All stock selections and investment ideas presented are based solely on the author's personal research, analysis, and opinion.

While every effort has been made to ensure the accuracy and reliability of the information provided, the author and publisher make no guarantees regarding the performance or potential returns of any stock mentioned in this book. There is no assurance that any investment or stock discussed will increase in value or result in profit. Investing in the stock market involves risk, and past performance is not indicative of future results.

Readers are solely responsible for their own investment decisions and are strongly encouraged to conduct their own research and consult with a qualified financial professional before making any financial or investment decisions. The author and publisher disclaim any liability for any loss or damages incurred, directly or indirectly, from the use of the information contained in this book.

Table of Contents

Introduction: Unlocking the Power of Undervalued Stocks

What if the next Amazon, Nvidia, or Tesla is currently trading for under $20, and you just haven't heard about it yet?

It's not a fantasy. It's happened before, and it's happening again. **Microsoft once traded under $1. Apple under $2. Netflix under $5.** These household names all had one thing in common before they exploded in value: they were overlooked. Most investors missed the window because they weren't looking in the right places or didn't know what to look for. That's where this book comes in.

In the world of investing, people often assume that higher stock prices mean higher quality. But **price alone tells you nothing about value**. A $15 stock can hold more explosive potential than a $300 stock; if you understand what makes it tick. And when you do? That's when the real opportunity begins.

Many retail investors make the same mistake: they chase hype, follow the herd, or rely on social media for their picks. They're bombarded with noise, speculation, and quick-money promises that rarely pan out. Worse, they often overlook the very stocks that have the most upside because those stocks don't have the flashiest headlines or cult followings (yet).

The truth is, most people don't know where to find quality companies that are *still affordable.* They either play it safe with overpriced blue chips, or gamble on high-risk penny stocks with no real business model. Both approaches can be dead ends if you're not careful.

What's missing is a smart, **research-driven approach to finding undervalued gems**: companies trading under $20 with legitimate potential to multiply in value.

This isn't a get-rich-quick guide. It's a deep dive into **20 real, publicly traded companies** with sound fundamentals, growing industries, and the potential to deliver outsized returns. I wrote this book with one bold promise in mind:

By the end of this book, you'll have a clear understanding of which low-priced stocks show the highest potential for 10x growth and why.

These aren't random picks or recycled favorites from social media. Every stock featured in this book was selected through **a disciplined research process** that evaluated fundamentals, market trends, innovation, leadership, and institutional sentiment.

Here's what you can expect to learn:

- What makes a stock a strong 10x candidate (hint: it's not just low price)

- How to spot undervalued opportunities before they gain mainstream attention

- Which sectors are primed for explosive growth over the next 3–5 years

- How to assess a company's real potential, even if it's flying under Wall Street's radar

You'll get a **detailed analysis of each stock**, including business model insights, competitive positioning, financial health, key catalysts, and the risks to be aware of. Whether you're a beginner looking to build your first high-upside portfolio or a seasoned investor searching for your next breakout opportunity, this book offers something real and actionable.

Why Focus on Stocks Under $20?

The price point matters: not because cheaper is better, but because **affordable stocks often slip through the cracks** of mainstream investment media. These companies may be in early growth stages, undergoing a turnaround, or simply misunderstood. Their valuations haven't caught up to their potential… yet.

That's where the upside lives. **If you can buy a stock at $10 and it grows to $100, that's not luck; that's strategy.** And while not every pick will be a 10x success, the goal is to give you exposure to the kind of asymmetric opportunities that can redefine your portfolio's trajectory.

Of course, with high upside comes risk. These stocks aren't without volatility, and they're not immune to market forces. That's why understanding **risk vs. reward** is essential. This book doesn't shy away from the risks; it addresses them head-on. You'll get the full picture so you can make **informed decisions**, not emotional ones.

Why You Can Trust What's Inside

I'm not a hedge fund manager or a TV pundit. I'm an independent researcher and investor who's spent years digging into markets, studying company filings, analyzing trends, and most importantly, putting my own money to work. My picks aren't theoretical; they come from the same due diligence I apply to my personal portfolio.

In this book, you'll benefit from countless hours of hands-on research. I don't rely on buzz or baseless predictions. I look for real signals: **undervalued financials, strong leadership, market momentum, product innovation, and institutional interest.** These are the elements that separate wishful thinking from strategic investing.

How This Book Is Structured

To make your reading experience as valuable and practical as possible, the book is broken into three parts:

- **Chapter 1-20** are the core: a breakdown of 20 stocks under $20 that show credible potential to multiply in value. Each stock gets its own chapter, with easy-to-understand analysis; even if you're not a financial expert.

- **Chapters 21**: takes a deeper dive into practical investing strategies. You'll learn how to identify low-priced stocks with genuine high-growth potential before they hit the mainstream. This chapter guides you through building a diversified portfolio using the 20 picks featured in this book, managing risk, setting position sizes, and developing strong research habits. It also equips you with the tools to continue discovering your own future 10x opportunities long after you've finished reading.

- **Conclusion**: wraps up the key lessons, encouraging you to think long-term, stay informed, and maintain a disciplined approach on your investing journey.

Throughout the book, I've made every effort to **explain concepts in simple, practical language**. You won't find unnecessary jargon, abstract theories, or bloated filler. Instead, you'll get clear analysis, real research, and actionable takeaways that you can apply whether you're investing $500 or $50,000.

My goal is to give you more than information; I want to give you insight. By the time you turn the final page, you'll know exactly what to look for in low-priced stocks, how to evaluate future opportunities with confidence, and which companies are positioned to shape the next wave of growth in 2025 and beyond.

Chapter 1: D-Wave Quantum Inc. – Ticker: QBTS

D-Wave Quantum Inc. (NYSE: QBTS) is a pioneering force in the quantum computing industry, focusing specifically on the development and commercialization of quantum annealing systems. While the broader quantum landscape is saturated with speculation and long-term potential, D-Wave has set itself apart by bringing practical, real-world applications to market. Its unique approach and functioning products make it a compelling case study in how quantum technology is starting to influence mainstream industries. As businesses seek out increasingly advanced methods for optimization, artificial intelligence, and complex problem modeling, D-Wave positions itself at a rare intersection of proven results and future-forward innovation.

Company Overview

Founded in 1999 and headquartered in British Columbia, Canada, D-Wave holds the distinction of being the first company to offer a commercially available quantum computer. It has since developed expertise in quantum annealing—a specialized subset of quantum computing designed to solve optimization problems more efficiently than classical computers. These problems include logistics optimization, financial forecasting, machine learning enhancements, and intelligent scheduling. While many companies in the quantum space are still in experimental or developmental phases, D-Wave has already deployed systems into the hands of paying enterprise customers.

Key components of D-Wave's business include:

- **Quantum Cloud Service (Leap™)**: A scalable cloud-based platform that provides users with remote access to D-Wave's quantum systems and advanced hybrid solvers. Leap allows developers and organizations to integrate quantum capabilities into their existing workflows.

- **Quantum Annealers**: These processors are optimized to tackle combinatorial optimization challenges—common in industries ranging from transportation to fintech—by evaluating countless possibilities and finding the most efficient outcomes.

- **Professional Services**: D-Wave also offers consulting and implementation services that help clients conceptualize, prototype, and operationalize quantum-driven solutions.

- **Next-Generation Hardware**: Ongoing development of Advantage2, a state-of-the-art quantum processing unit (QPU), is expected to dramatically improve scalability, problem complexity handling, and solution accuracy.

What Makes QBTS Stand Out

D-Wave's commercial-first, application-centric strategy makes it a rare outlier in a field dominated by academic research and long R&D timelines:

- **Real Revenue and Real-World Usage**: D-Wave has an expanding portfolio of corporate customers, including high-profile names like Volkswagen, Lockheed Martin, Mastercard, and Deloitte. These partnerships validate the company's technology and business model.

- **Focused Market Position**: Instead of trying to be everything to everyone, D-Wave's focus on optimization through quantum annealing allows it to dominate a clearly defined and high-demand segment.

- **First-Mover Advantage**: With over two decades of specialized quantum R&D, D-Wave has not only built sophisticated technology but also cultivated key industry relationships and institutional knowledge that give it a long-term edge.

- **Hybrid Architecture**: By blending classical and quantum approaches, D-Wave's systems offer immediate value even when full-scale quantum dominance remains years away. This hybridization bridges today's needs with tomorrow's possibilities.

Why It's Undervalued

Despite its technological achievements and increasing commercial traction, QBTS trades at a valuation that appears to ignore its unique position in a trillion-dollar computing market:

- **Quantum Misconceptions**: Many investors misunderstand D-Wave's business model or incorrectly group it with pre-revenue, purely speculative ventures, which downplays its commercial momentum.

- **Tech Sector Skepticism**: Broader bearish sentiment around unprofitable tech companies has clouded investor perception, even when real-world adoption exists.

- **Lack of Retail Awareness**: D-Wave remains obscure for many retail investors, partly due to limited media coverage and analyst attention, despite numerous success stories and credible partnerships.

Multiple data points support a bullish case:

- **Growing Commercial Adoption**: More enterprise clients are integrating D-Wave's hybrid solvers, driving quarter-over-quarter revenue growth and building long-term customer dependency.

- **Innovative Hardware Roadmap**: The upcoming Advantage2 QPU could dramatically expand D-

Wave's capabilities, opening doors to higher-value contracts and deeper client integrations.

- **Strategic Collaborations**: Partnerships with Amazon Web Services, Accenture, and NEC provide technological validation, operational scale, and global distribution networks.

10x Potential Catalyst

D-Wave could see explosive growth over the next five to ten years if the following catalysts play out:

- **Quantum-as-a-Service (QaaS) Growth**: Leap's cloud-based, usage-driven revenue model mirrors successful SaaS paradigms, offering D-Wave recurring and scalable income.

- **Government Adoption**: Departments focused on logistics, defense, energy, and research could fuel massive contracts as quantum capabilities prove mission-critical.

- **AI and Quantum Convergence**: By helping optimize machine learning models, D-Wave's quantum systems could play a major role in accelerating AI across sectors.

- **Advantage2 Rollout**: The successful commercial deployment of this advanced QPU may demonstrate practical quantum supremacy within specific use cases, accelerating market penetration and investor enthusiasm.

Financial Overview

- **Revenue Growth**: Although still in early stages, revenue has consistently increased, backed by real enterprise usage and expanding client demand.

- **Cash Flow and Burn**: Like many deep-tech companies, D-Wave operates at a high burn rate due to ongoing R&D and hardware investment, but this is aligned with the company's long-term vision.

- **Improving Margins**: Gross margins are gradually improving as software solutions scale and hybrid solvers reduce reliance on expensive infrastructure.

- **Robust Pipeline**: A growing sales pipeline and backlog of enterprise projects offer visibility into future revenue acceleration.

Risks to Consider

- **Quantum Field Volatility**: The broader quantum space is inherently volatile, with rapidly evolving benchmarks, making it difficult to forecast long-term winners.

- **High Capital Needs**: The capital-intensive nature of building and maintaining quantum hardware may necessitate ongoing fundraising and the potential dilution of existing shareholders.

- **Customer Education Curve**: Many organizations are unfamiliar with quantum computing, which could lengthen adoption timelines and slow growth.

- **Competitive Pressure**: Tech giants like IBM, Google, and Microsoft are heavily investing in quantum, making the competitive environment fierce and dynamic.

Wall Street Sentiment & Insider Activity

- **Growing Analyst Interest**: As quantum computing garners mainstream recognition, QBTS is beginning to appear on more institutional radars.

- **Strong Insider Confidence**: High levels of insider ownership, including founding members and long-term executives, reflect deep commitment and belief in the company's trajectory.

- **ETF Momentum**: Potential inclusion in AI, quantum, or deep-tech themed ETFs could dramatically boost visibility and trading volume for QBTS.

Final Verdict

D-Wave Quantum Inc. is not just a speculative quantum computing company; it's a commercial trailblazer delivering tangible results to real-world clients. Its singular focus on quantum annealing, hybrid architecture, and an expanding enterprise client base position it as a standout in the next generation of computing. For investors willing to weather volatility in exchange for high-upside potential, QBTS offers an attractive entry point into a future-defining technology. As the quantum narrative matures and practical deployments become more widespread, D-Wave has the potential to evolve from a niche player into a core component of the enterprise technology stack.

Chapter 2: ACM Research Inc. – Ticker: ACMR

ACM Research (NASDAQ: ACMR) is a lesser-known yet increasingly pivotal player in the semiconductor equipment industry. The company designs, develops, and manufactures wafer processing solutions used in the production of integrated circuits. As the global demand for semiconductors continues to surge, ACMR's innovative technology positions it as a high-growth contender in a critical supply chain segment. Its proprietary cleaning tools and advanced packaging solutions are gaining traction among leading semiconductor manufacturers in China and beyond

Company Overview

Founded in 1998 and headquartered in Fremont, California, ACM Research focuses on equipment used in front-end semiconductor processing—specifically, wet cleaning and surface preparation tools. The company's product lineup is tailored to meet the demands of advanced semiconductor nodes, making its solutions increasingly vital as chip geometries shrink and process complexity grows.

ACMR operates through several key product lines:

- **Single-Wafer Wet Cleaning Equipment**: The company's core product line, which includes tools designed for ultra-clean wafer surfaces, critical to defect reduction and yield improvement.

- **Bevel Etch and Scrubbing Systems**: These systems are integral for edge-bead removal and particle elimination, ensuring device reliability and process consistency.

- **Advanced Packaging Equipment**: ACMR has recently expanded into tools that support 3D packaging, a rapidly growing segment of the semiconductor industry.

Although most of ACMR's revenue comes from China—a country heavily investing in semiconductor self-sufficiency—it is gradually expanding its customer base across Asia and entering the U.S. and European markets. The company also has a majority stake in ACM Research (Shanghai), a Chinese subsidiary that plays a critical role in manufacturing and R&D.

Why It's Undervalued

Despite its strong fundamentals and niche market leadership, ACMR trades at a significant discount compared to U.S.-based peers like Lam Research (LRCX) or Applied Materials (AMAT). The primary reason for this undervaluation is geopolitical risk. Concerns over U.S.-China relations and export restrictions have caused many investors to shy away from companies with heavy exposure to China. However, this risk has led to a market mispricing that creates a compelling opportunity for informed, risk-tolerant investors.

Several factors support the undervaluation thesis:

- **Strong Growth Despite Headwinds**: ACMR has continued to post revenue growth even amid heightened U.S.-China tensions and global semiconductor supply chain disruptions.

- **Proprietary Technology**: Its differentiated approach to wet cleaning, which uses high-velocity particle removal rather than traditional batch immersion, offers superior cleaning efficiency for advanced chips.

- **Low Valuation Multiples**: The stock trades at a forward P/E ratio and price-to-sales ratio well below the industry average, suggesting ample room for multiple expansion.

10x Growth Thesis

ACMR's long-term potential is rooted in the explosive growth of the semiconductor industry and the increasing complexity of chip manufacturing.

- **Massive TAM Expansion**: The company is addressing a total addressable market that could exceed $20 billion by 2030 as semiconductor manufacturing scales up to meet AI, 5G, and high-performance computing demands.

- **Localization Tailwinds in China**: With China doubling down on semiconductor independence, ACMR stands to benefit from increased demand for locally sourced equipment.

- **Product Portfolio Expansion**: The launch of new tools for 3D packaging, vertical stacking, and hybrid bonding technologies positions ACMR at the forefront of next-generation chip architecture.

- **Capacity and Global Reach**: ACMR is ramping up manufacturing capacity and has initiated plans for a new R&D center in South Korea, signaling its intent to diversify geographically.

- **Margins and Operating Leverage**: As the company scales, its margins are expected to expand, driven by higher average selling prices, increased automation, and economies of scale.

Key Financial Highlights

ACMR's financials reflect strong execution, disciplined growth, and improving profitability metrics.

- **Revenue Growth**: ACMR reported $530 million in revenue for the trailing twelve months, a 34% increase year-over-year. This sustained growth is fueled by strong demand for wafer cleaning and packaging tools.

- **Earnings Growth**: Net income reached $72 million in the most recent fiscal year, with a net profit margin of over 13% and increasing operating efficiency.

- **Cash Position**: The company has over $320 million in cash and short-term investments, providing ample resources for R&D and expansion.

- **Low Debt**: ACMR has minimal long-term debt, with a debt-to-equity ratio under 0.2, reflecting a conservative and flexible capital structure.

- **Valuation Ratios**:

  ○ Price-to-Sales (P/S): ~2.5

  ○ Forward Price-to-Earnings (P/E): ~14

  ○ Price-to-Book (P/B): ~2.3 These ratios are far below industry leaders, suggesting significant upside if investor sentiment improves.

Risks to Watch

While ACMR has strong fundamentals, several risks could affect its investment thesis.

- **Geopolitical Risk**: Trade tensions, export bans, or escalating restrictions could hinder ACMR's operations in China or limit access to foreign markets.

- **Customer Concentration**: A significant portion of ACMR's revenue is derived from a handful of customers, increasing vulnerability to demand shifts.

- **Technology Competition**: Larger players with deeper R&D budgets could develop competing products, pressuring ACMR to innovate continuously.

- **Market Cyclicality**: The semiconductor industry is cyclical, and downturns can lead to order deferrals or cancellations.

Analyst Ratings & Insider Sentiment

- **Wall Street Analysts**: Most analysts covering ACMR rate it a "Buy" due to its solid earnings track record and strong product positioning.

- **Target Price Range**: Consensus price targets range from $22 to $30, suggesting considerable upside from its current sub-$20 price.

- **Insider Ownership**: Founders and executives hold a meaningful stake in the company, aligning their interests with shareholders.

- **Institutional Investment**: Major firms including BlackRock and Fidelity have increased their positions in ACMR, signaling growing institutional confidence.

Final Verdict

ACM Research is a hidden gem in the semiconductor ecosystem. Its cutting-edge wafer cleaning and packaging tools are critical to the ongoing miniaturization and sophistication of chip design. Despite geopolitical headwinds, ACMR has executed consistently and expanded both revenue and earnings.

What makes ACMR particularly attractive is the combination of undervaluation, strong balance sheet, and exposure to a structurally growing industry. Its stock remains under the radar, which allows savvy investors to accumulate shares before broader market recognition.

For investors seeking a high-potential semiconductor play under $20, ACMR delivers a compelling blend of innovation, financial strength, and long-term relevance. If management continues to deliver and geopolitical risks are managed or discounted, ACMR could easily be a 10x stock over the next decade.

Chapter 3: SoFi Technologies Inc. – Ticker: SOFI

SoFi Technologies (NASDAQ: SOFI) is one of the most recognized and rapidly evolving fintech companies in the United States. Its mission is to help individuals achieve financial independence by offering a diverse suite of digital financial services. These include lending, investing, banking, credit card services, and personal finance management tools—all integrated into a single user-friendly platform. SoFi has designed an all-in-one financial ecosystem that resonates particularly with millennials and Gen Z consumers who prefer managing their finances through modern digital channels rather than through legacy banking institutions.

Company Overview

Founded in 2011 as a student loan refinancing platform, SoFi has transformed into a comprehensive fintech powerhouse. The company now operates across three main business segments: Lending, Financial Services, and Technology Platform.

- **Lending** is the foundation of SoFi's revenue model and includes personal loans, student loan refinancing, and home loans. These products are increasingly attractive due to the company's competitive interest rates and user-centric digital experience.

- **Financial Services** encompasses a range of offerings like SoFi Money (cash management account), SoFi Invest (platform for stocks, ETFs, and cryptocurrencies), SoFi Credit Card, and SoFi Relay (budgeting and financial tracking tool). These services are designed to engage users at every stage of their financial journey.

- **Technology Platform** is primarily driven by Galileo, a backend infrastructure provider acquired by SoFi. Galileo powers fintech apps and digital banks, providing SoFi with a steady, scalable revenue stream that is not directly tied to its consumer-facing operations.

SoFi operates a digital-first business model that reaches customers via its mobile application and online portal. In 2022, it obtained a national bank charter, enhancing its operational efficiency and ability to directly manage deposits and issue loans. This charter also allows SoFi to earn more per loan originated, since it eliminates reliance on third-party banks.

Why It's Undervalued

At its current market price, SoFi appears significantly undervalued when compared to its intrinsic worth and relative to other players in the fintech space. Over the past two years, the stock has fluctuated between $4 and $25, with the present lower valuation offering a compelling entry point for long-term investors.

Several external factors have contributed to this price compression. Broad market sentiment around fintech has soured due to macroeconomic headwinds like interest rate hikes, inflation, and regulatory uncertainty. However, despite these pressures, SoFi has demonstrated steady revenue growth and user base expansion. It's also one of the few fintech firms in its price range to achieve GAAP profitability—a major milestone that reflects operational strength.

Unlike many fintech companies that either bleed cash or rely on speculative business models, SoFi has built a balanced, sustainable operation. When compared with peers such as Robinhood (HOOD) and Block (SQ), SoFi trades at a lower price-to-sales ratio while offering a more diversified and resilient business structure.

10x Growth Thesis

SoFi's potential to deliver 10x returns lies in its ambition to become a dominant financial super app—a platform where users can meet all their financial needs under one roof. The combination of customer-facing services and backend infrastructure makes the business highly scalable.

- **Business Model Scalability**: The company's integrated ecosystem facilitates growth through cross-selling. As customers enter through one product—such as a personal loan—they are often introduced to other services, increasing the average revenue per user. The bank charter further improves profitability by lowering funding costs.

- **Technological Advantage**: Through Galileo, SoFi supports a large number of fintechs and neobanks. As demand for embedded finance grows, Galileo's client base is likely to expand, adding a high-margin revenue stream.

- **Disruptive Positioning**: SoFi challenges traditional banks by offering faster service, more transparency, lower fees, and a superior digital interface. By consolidating everything from loans to investments to credit cards, SoFi simplifies the user experience in ways that traditional banks struggle to replicate.

- **Catalysts for Growth**:
  - Continued expansion of SoFi Invest, potentially including new asset classes and investment tools.

  - Monetization of its growing user base through premium offerings.

  - Increasing adoption of Galileo by other financial platforms.

  - Strategic partnerships and product integrations.

  - Strong organic user acquisition, with over 8.1 million members as of Q1 2025 and more than 1 million new members added during that quarter alone.

Key Financial Highlights

The financial performance of SoFi indicates robust fundamentals rarely seen in fintech companies trading under $20.

- **Revenue Growth**: Revenue for the trailing twelve months exceeded $2.2 billion, reflecting a compound annual growth rate (CAGR) of more than 40% since 2021. This consistent expansion speaks to the strength of both the Lending and Technology Platform segments.

- **Profitability Milestone**: SoFi reported GAAP net income profitability in Q4 2023 and has maintained positive earnings into 2025. This shift to profitability marks a significant turning point for investor confidence.

- **Cash Reserves**: The company holds over $2.5 billion in cash and cash equivalents as of Q1 2025, providing a substantial liquidity cushion for future growth initiatives and weathering market volatility.

- **Debt and Leverage**: SoFi maintains a conservative debt profile, with a debt-to-equity ratio around 0.4—far below the fintech industry average. This demonstrates prudent capital management.

- **Valuation Ratios**:
  - Price-to-Sales (P/S): ~3.1
  - Forward Price-to-Earnings (P/E): ~32

o   Price-to-Book (P/B): ~1.5

These ratios suggest SoFi is trading at a justifiable valuation, especially considering its consistent revenue growth and recently achieved profitability.

Risks to Watch

Although SoFi is a promising investment, it's essential to be aware of potential risks that could impact its growth trajectory.

- **Competitive Pressure**: The fintech landscape is intensely competitive, with both startups and traditional financial institutions vying for market share. SoFi will need to continue innovating to maintain its edge.

- **Regulatory Landscape**: As a chartered bank and public fintech company, SoFi is under close regulatory supervision. Any tightening of financial regulations or changes in consumer protection laws could affect operations.

- **Operational Complexity**: Managing multiple high-growth business lines simultaneously introduces complexity, and scaling too fast could lead to service degradation or inefficiencies.

- **Macroeconomic Factors**: Interest rate shifts, inflation, and economic downturns could influence consumer borrowing and investment behavior, affecting SoFi's revenue streams.

Analyst Ratings & Insider Sentiment

The overall sentiment among Wall Street analysts is optimistic, particularly following the company's transition to profitability.

- **Average Analyst Rating**: "Buy" or "Outperform," with an emphasis on the company's diversified revenue model and margin expansion.

- **Target Price Range**: Between $10 and $14, representing meaningful upside potential from the current trading price.

- **Insider Activity**: CEO Anthony Noto has made multiple significant purchases of SoFi shares in the open market, a strong indicator of confidence in the company's prospects.

- **Institutional Ownership**: Over 60% of SoFi's outstanding shares are held by major institutions, including Vanguard, BlackRock, and Morgan Stanley. This level of ownership often reflects confidence in the company's long-term outlook.

Final Verdict

SoFi Technologies has successfully positioned itself as a next-generation financial services provider that blends modern convenience with banking reliability. It stands out not just for its rapid growth but for the solid foundation it has built—profitability, diversified revenue, and scalable infrastructure.

What earns SoFi a place in the top 20 stocks under $20 is its rare combination of innovation, discipline, and execution. It is not merely a speculative bet, but a calculated investment in the future of finance. Unlike many of its fintech peers that continue to struggle with profitability or rely on narrow revenue streams, SoFi has demonstrated it can scale responsibly while delivering real shareholder value.

With a moderate risk profile, strong financial fundamentals, and a multi-faceted growth strategy, SoFi is poised to reward patient investors over a 3 to 5-year horizon. Its potential to become a dominant force in consumer and embedded finance makes it one of the most compelling fintech investments available today.

Chapter 4: SoundHound AI Inc. – Ticker: SOUN

SoundHound AI Inc. (NASDAQ: SOUN) is a cutting-edge innovator in the rapidly growing and highly competitive field of voice artificial intelligence. The company has developed a proprietary voice AI platform that supports natural, human-like conversational interactions with technology. Its scalable, modular solution is now being used across multiple industries, such as automotive, consumer electronics, customer service, and hospitality. As voice interfaces emerge as the next major wave in human-computer interaction, SOUN represents a particularly intriguing and undervalued investment opportunity under $10, with the potential for significant long-term upside.

Company Overview

Founded in 2005 and headquartered in Santa Clara, California, SoundHound began its journey as a music recognition app, akin to Shazam. Over the years, the company has undergone a major transformation to become a full-stack AI-driven voice platform provider. Its advanced technology stack is built around natural language understanding (NLU), automatic speech recognition (ASR), and deep meaning understanding (DMU), allowing systems to interpret, understand, and respond to human voice commands in real time with high accuracy.

At the heart of SoundHound's innovation is "Houndify," the company's signature voice AI development platform. Houndify is engineered to be highly flexible and customizable, enabling developers and businesses to embed sophisticated voice interfaces into their products without ceding control or data to dominant tech giants like Amazon, Apple, or Google. Supporting more than 25 languages and dialects, Houndify is now present in millions of vehicles, consumer devices, and enterprise systems globally.

SoundHound offers a wide range of voice AI applications and services, including:

- **Voice AI for Automotive**: Adopted by leading global automakers such as Hyundai, Mercedes-Benz, and Honda, providing intelligent in-car voice assistants for controlling navigation, climate settings, entertainment systems, and more.

- **Smart Device Integration**: Embedded in various Internet of Things (IoT) devices like smart speakers, kitchen appliances, and wearable tech, allowing hands-free control and smarter user experiences.

- **Customer Service Automation**: Powering conversational AI for businesses in hospitality, QSR (quick-service restaurants), and customer support, helping them automate interactions, reduce operational costs, and enhance customer satisfaction.

Why It's Undervalued

Despite its technological leadership and promising business model, SOUN remains significantly undervalued in the public markets. Its relatively recent public debut through a SPAC merger in 2022 has contributed to its low investor visibility. Combined with general skepticism toward small-cap AI companies, this has created a rare entry point for early investors.

Several key points underscore this undervaluation:

- **Strong Strategic Partnerships**: Collaborations with industry leaders such as Hyundai, Snap, Toast, and Qualcomm illustrate the widespread and growing demand for SoundHound's capabilities across different verticals.

- **Recurring Revenue Model**: The company is increasingly shifting toward subscription-based and licensing revenue, providing greater predictability and financial stability.

- **Small Market Cap**: With a current market capitalization under $1 billion, SoundHound trades at a steep discount relative to its technological peers, many of which have less proven commercial traction.

10x Growth Thesis

SoundHound's long-term investment case is built around its potential to capture a significant share of the booming voice AI market. Several catalysts could drive its valuation up by 10x or more over the next decade:

- **Expanding Total Addressable Market (TAM)**: The global voice AI market is forecast to surpass $50 billion by 2030, with demand fueled by the proliferation of virtual assistants, automation, and smart devices.

- **Edge Computing Advantage**: SoundHound supports voice AI at the edge, eliminating the need for constant internet connectivity. This allows for faster, more private, and more reliable voice interaction—ideal for automotive and embedded device use cases.

- **Data Ownership and Privacy Focus**: Unlike big tech alternatives, SoundHound allows clients to retain ownership of user data. This aligns with increasing regulatory scrutiny and demand for data sovereignty.

- **Restaurant Automation Surge**: One of SoundHound's fastest-growing verticals is its Voice AI for QSRs. The solution is already being rolled out in drive-thrus, phone systems, and kiosks across major fast-food chains, unlocking massive productivity gains.

- **Global Expansion Momentum**: With partnerships extending across North America, Europe, the Middle East, and Asia, SoundHound is well on its way to becoming a truly global AI platform provider.

Key Financial Highlights

Though still in the early stages of full monetization, SoundHound's financials show strong signs of progress and future potential:

- **Revenue Acceleration**: Generated $45 million in revenue in 2023, reflecting nearly 80% growth year-over-year, indicating increasing enterprise demand and product adoption.

- **Robust Backlog**: Holds over $350 million in contracted revenue backlog, offering visibility into long-term cash flow and customer retention.

- **Improving Margins**: Gross margins have improved to over 65%, supported by high-value contracts and greater operational efficiency.

- **Strong Cash Position**: Closed 2023 with $110 million in cash reserves, providing ample runway for R&D, hiring, and global expansion.

- **Operational Efficiency**: Operating losses are decreasing steadily as the company scales revenue and manages costs.

Risks to Watch

Every investment carries risk, and SoundHound is no exception. Investors should be mindful of the following potential challenges:

- **Competitive Landscape**: The company faces stiff competition from tech behemoths like Amazon (Alexa), Google (Assistant), and Apple (Siri), all of which have larger marketing budgets and ecosystems.

- **Client Concentration**: A significant portion of SoundHound's revenue is concentrated among a few key clients. Loss of any one of them could materially impact short-term earnings.

- **Execution & Scalability**: Managing rapid growth while maintaining the high standards of accuracy, latency, and reliability in voice recognition is technically demanding.

- **Perception as a SPAC**: As a recent SPAC entity, it may still face skepticism among institutional investors until it demonstrates consistent profitability.

Analyst Ratings & Insider Sentiment

- **Wall Street Sentiment**: A majority of analysts covering SOUN rate it a "Buy" or "Outperform," citing its differentiated technology and growing adoption across industries.

- **Valuation Outlook**: Price targets range from $5 to $8 per share, reflecting a strong upside from current trading levels.

- **Insider Confidence**: Company founders and executives continue to hold substantial equity stakes, suggesting confidence in the long-term vision and alignment with shareholder interests.

- **Institutional Endorsements**: Respected investment firms like Vanguard and BlackRock have taken positions in SOUN, lending further credibility to the company's outlook.

Final Verdict

SoundHound AI Inc. is uniquely positioned at the intersection of AI, voice interaction, and enterprise digital transformation. With nearly two decades of research and development, a robust and flexible voice AI platform, and increasing enterprise traction, the company is poised to become a cornerstone of the next-generation AI economy.

Despite current undervaluation, SoundHound boasts a growing revenue base, substantial backlog, and strong strategic partnerships. As more devices and industries embrace voice as a primary interface, SoundHound is likely to power a significant portion of that interaction layer.

For investors seeking exposure to a niche yet rapidly expanding corner of AI under $20, SOUN offers a high-reward profile. If the company continues to execute on its vision and scale effectively, a 10x return is not just a possibility—it's a realistic scenario backed by market trends, customer demand, and technological excellence.

Chapter 5: Nintendo Co., Ltd. – Ticker: NTDOY

Nintendo (OTC: NTDOY) is not just a gaming company. It's a cultural juggernaut, a storytelling empire, and a cash-flow machine disguised as a nostalgic brand. While many investors chase AI and biotech trends, Nintendo offers something rare in today's market: enduring IP, loyal global audiences, and a rock-solid balance sheet. Priced under $20, NTDOY represents a chance to own a legacy tech company with the DNA of a startup and the reach of a multinational.

Company Overview

Founded in 1889 and headquartered in Kyoto, Japan, Nintendo has evolved from a playing card company into one of the most recognized names in global entertainment. Its intellectual property catalog—featuring names like Mario, Zelda, Donkey Kong, and Pokemon—has proven timeless, resilient, and cross-generational.

What makes Nintendo unique is its ability to reinvent itself without losing its soul. Whether it's the Wii, the DS, or the Nintendo Switch, the company has repeatedly disrupted the gaming space by focusing on creativity, accessibility, and innovation over raw specs. The upcoming "Switch 2" is expected to build on this legacy, attracting both hardcore fans and casual gamers alike.

Nintendo also owns stakes in The Pokemon Company and has expanded into films, theme parks (in partnership with Universal Studios), and mobile games. The recent success of "The Super Mario Bros. Movie" signals a broader multimedia strategy to monetize its IP across platforms.

Why It's Undervalued

Despite these massive tailwinds, NTDOY is trading at a valuation that fails to capture its full potential.

- **Strong Balance Sheet**: Over $12 billion in cash and zero debt. Nintendo can invest aggressively without financial strain.

- **Conservative Valuation**: Trades at a forward P/E ratio significantly lower than most tech or gaming peers.

- **IP-Driven Business**: Unlike most gaming companies, Nintendo doesn't rent its characters. It owns them, merchandises them, and builds empires around them.

- **Recurring Revenue Potential**: With Nintendo Switch Online and digital sales increasing, Nintendo is quietly building a subscription-style ecosystem.

Investors focused only on hardware cycles miss the bigger picture. Nintendo is transitioning from a device company to a content-and-experiences powerhouse.

The 10x Growth Thesis

Nintendo's future isn't just about the next console. It's about turning beloved IP into an integrated, global entertainment universe.

- **Switch Successor Momentum**: The anticipated next-gen console is expected to launch in 2025, renewing hardware and software sales.

- **Digital Sales Boom**: Digital downloads now make up more than half of Nintendo's software revenue, with high margins and repeat engagement.

- **Multimedia Expansion**: More movies are in the pipeline. Think Disney-style content rollouts featuring Nintendo characters.

- **Theme Parks**: Super Nintendo World attractions are expanding beyond Japan and Hollywood. These parks create brand immersion and long-tail revenue.

- **Mobile Monetization**: Nintendo's cautious mobile approach is now yielding results through games like Fire Emblem Heroes and Mario Kart Tour.

- **Emerging Markets**: Growing penetration in Latin America and Southeast Asia presents a large untapped user base.

Combine all these with a fanbase that spans generations and you have the foundation for a global IP engine capable of exponential growth.

Financial Highlights

Nintendo's fundamentals remain outstanding:

- **FY 2023 Revenue**: $12.1 billion, with consistent profitability.

- **Operating Margin**: Nearly 30%, showing efficiency in content creation.

- **ROE**: Around 15%, reflecting strong returns on equity.

- **Cash Reserves**: $12+ billion with no long-term debt.

- **Dividends**: Consistently pays dividends (approximately 1.24% annually), providing yield for long-term holders.

Nintendo's conservative management style ensures sustainability, while its product pipeline suggests meaningful upside.

Risks to Consider

- **Hardware Dependency**: Sales can fluctuate based on console cycles.

- **Pacing of Content**: Nintendo's slow release schedule can frustrate investors seeking short-term growth.

- **Limited M&A Activity**: Unlike competitors, Nintendo rarely makes acquisitions, potentially missing external growth opportunities.

- **Currency Fluctuations**: As a Japanese company, profits can be affected by yen volatility.

These risks are real but manageable, especially given Nintendo's loyal fanbase and diverse monetization channels.

Analyst Sentiment & Insider Perspective

- **Wall Street Analysts**: Most rate NTDOY as a "Buy" or "Strong Buy," citing its stable cash flow and underappreciated IP value.

- **Institutional Holders**: Major funds like Fidelity and Capital Group have increased their stakes in recent quarters.

- **Insider Confidence**: The founding Yamauchi family's continued influence underscores long-term vision over short-term noise.

Final Verdict

Nintendo isn't just a gaming company—it's a multi-platform IP empire in disguise. With a pristine balance sheet, iconic franchises, and expanding revenue streams, NTDOY offers investors a unique blend of safety and upside.

With a stock price hovering around the $20 mark, NTDOY is a rare opportunity to own a piece of a global brand with the potential to 10x as it expands beyond gaming into full-spectrum entertainment. For those seeking a low-risk, high-reward stock that bridges tech, media, and consumer sectors, Nintendo is a no-brainer.

The next wave of entertainment will be driven by companies with deep IP, loyal audiences, and multiplatform reach. Nintendo checks all those boxes—and then some.

Chapter 6: Webull Corp. – Ticker: BULL

Webull Corp. (NASDAQ: BULL) is fast becoming a significant player in the fintech and online brokerage arena. While dominant names like Robinhood and Charles Schwab frequently capture the headlines, Webull is quietly building a formidable reputation through its data-driven platform, advanced trading tools, and aggressive international expansion. As the trend of retail investing accelerates worldwide, Webull's focus on empowering users through innovative features and educational tools positions BULL as an intriguing under-the-radar stock with substantial long-term growth potential.

Company Overview

Launched in 2017 and headquartered in New York City, Webull has quickly transformed from a niche trading app into a mainstream fintech contender. Initially appealing to tech-savvy traders, the platform now serves a broad demographic, offering commission-free trading on stocks, ETFs, options, and cryptocurrencies. Its sleek, user-friendly interface is available across both mobile and desktop platforms, making sophisticated investing tools accessible to a global audience.

Webull's mission is centered on democratizing finance and closing the gap between professional traders and retail investors. By delivering advanced features at no cost, Webull appeals to millennial and Gen Z investors who expect more from their trading experience.

Key features and services include:

- **Zero-Commission Trading**: Trade U.S. stocks, ETFs, and options without traditional fees.

- **Cryptocurrency Access**: Round-the-clock crypto trading with competitive spreads.

- **Advanced Technical Analysis Tools**: Includes real-time data, customizable charts, technical indicators, and Level 2 quotes.

- **Paper Trading Simulator**: Practice trades using simulated money to refine strategies without risk.

- **Extended Market Access**: Pre-market and after-hours trading is supported.

- **Smart Alerts and Screeners**: Customizable watchlists and alerts based on technical and fundamental criteria.

- **Fractional Shares and Retirement Accounts**: Enabling users to invest in high-priced stocks and plan for the future.

Why It's Undervalued

Despite impressive growth metrics and user engagement, BULL remains relatively undervalued in the eyes of the market. The platform is often mistakenly lumped in with unproven or speculative fintech startups, when in reality, it has established a robust operational foundation, proven user traction, and a diversified revenue model.

Several factors underscore this undervaluation:

- **Aggressive International Expansion**: With launches in Australia, the UK, and Singapore, Webull is tapping into untapped markets with high growth potential.

- **Sticky User Base**: Thanks to powerful tools and a gamified experience, Webull enjoys high engagement and user retention.

- **Multiple Revenue Streams**: Monetization from payment for order flow, margin interest, premium data packages, lending services, and idle cash interest.

- **Minimal Institutional Ownership**: Still early in public market visibility, increased institutional investment could catalyze price appreciation.

- **Strong Brand Equity**: Webull's reputation for providing institutional-grade tools has built strong brand loyalty among tech-forward investors.

10x Growth Thesis

Webull's differentiated platform, combined with favorable macro trends, supports a strong case for 10x potential over the next decade.

- **Mainstreaming of Retail Investing**: Retail investors now account for a substantial portion of daily volume on U.S. exchanges. Webull is well-positioned to serve this demographic with enhanced tools and educational content.

- **Tech-Driven Value Proposition**: Unlike minimalist competitors, Webull offers rich functionality that appeals to both beginners and advanced users.

- **Youth-Centric Appeal**: A large percentage of Webull's user base is under 35, aligning with long-term investing horizons and compound growth potential.

- **Integrated Asset Offering**: The ability to trade equities, options, and crypto on a single platform satisfies the demands of modern investors.

- **Upcoming Product Launches**: Planned introductions of retirement accounts, portfolio analysis tools, and social trading features could further boost engagement.

- **Strategic Partnerships**: Collaborations with backend providers, banks, and educational institutions will expand Webull's ecosystem and functionality.

- **Global Compliance Strategy**: Webull is proactively navigating regulatory frameworks across multiple jurisdictions, ensuring long-term sustainability.

Key Financial Highlights

Webull is transitioning from growth mode to sustainable scalability, with financial indicators suggesting a solid path toward profitability.

- **User Growth**: Surpassed 20 million global registered users by early 2024, reflecting strong market adoption.

- **Revenue Trajectory**: Estimated $600 million in revenue for 2023, up over 70% year-over-year, driven by increased trading volume and premium services.

- **Profitability Outlook**: Projected positive EBITDA by late 2025, aided by operating leverage and margin improvements.

- **Cash Reserves**: Holds over $300 million in cash, providing ample runway for R&D, marketing, and market expansion.

- **ARPU Trends**: Average revenue per user is rising, supported by the introduction of premium tools and expanded asset classes.

- **Operational Efficiency**: Improved cost structures and technology upgrades have resulted in reduced overhead per user.

Risks to Watch

Like any high-growth fintech company, Webull faces risks that must be considered by potential investors:

- **Crowded Market**: The brokerage space is highly competitive, with incumbents and new entrants vying for user attention.

- **Revenue Sensitivity**: Revenue is partially dependent on market activity, which can slow during downturns.

- **Regulatory Risk**: New rules around payment for order flow or crypto trading could affect business models.

- **Cybersecurity**: As a digital-first platform, Webull must continuously invest in cybersecurity to protect user data.

- **Platform Reliability**: Outages or glitches during high-volume trading could damage trust and lead to user attrition.

Analyst Ratings & Insider Sentiment

- **Wall Street Analysts**: Coverage remains limited but growing. Initial ratings highlight Webull's potential to capture significant market share.

- **Price Target Range**: Early analyst estimates suggest price targets between $8 and $14, reflecting upside potential from current levels.

- **Insider Ownership**: Founders and executives continue to hold meaningful equity, ensuring strong alignment with shareholders.

- **Institutional Investors**: Participation from fintech-focused funds is rising as Webull's metrics strengthen.

Final Verdict

Webull Corp. is building more than just a trading app—it's constructing the future of personal finance. By combining a powerful feature set with intuitive design and a strong global strategy, Webull stands out in a crowded market. It has shown that it can scale efficiently, attract and retain users, and develop innovative solutions that resonate with a new generation of investors.

For investors looking to gain exposure to the transformation of retail investing, BULL offers a rare mix of advanced technology, growth momentum, and market mispricing. The company's trajectory, driven by user-centric innovation and strategic international moves, positions it for explosive growth.

With strong fundamentals, visionary leadership, and a unique market position, BULL could easily outperform expectations. If Webull successfully continues its expansion and deepens user engagement, a 10x return may not only be possible—it could prove to be a conservative estimate.

Chapter 7: Rocket Lab USA, Inc. – Ticker: RKLB

Rocket Lab USA, Inc. (NASDAQ: RKLB) is rapidly emerging as one of the most intriguing and dynamic pure-play space companies available on public markets. While household names like SpaceX garner the lion's share of media attention, Rocket Lab has been methodically building an impressive track record, carving out a leadership position in small satellite launches and end-to-end space infrastructure services. For investors seeking asymmetric upside in the commercial space economy, RKLB presents a compelling, albeit high-risk, opportunity with the potential for explosive growth.

Company Overview

Founded in 2006 by visionary engineer Peter Beck in New Zealand, Rocket Lab was born out of a mission to make space more accessible, affordable, and frequent. What started as a niche aerospace startup has evolved into a formidable player in the global space race. The company's flagship launch vehicle, the Electron rocket, made history in 2017 by becoming the first private rocket launched from the Southern Hemisphere. Since then, Rocket Lab has completed over 40 successful missions, deploying more than 170 satellites for an array of commercial, research, and governmental clients.

Rocket Lab is far more than just a rocket company. Through strategic acquisitions and in-house development, the company has built out a vertically integrated space business. This means it now offers capabilities that span the entire value chain—from satellite component manufacturing to in-orbit operations. With the development of the Photon satellite platform, and the Neutron rocket for medium-lift payloads, Rocket Lab is positioning itself as a comprehensive provider for the booming space services industry.

Key features and services include:

- **Electron Rocket**: A lightweight, expendable launch vehicle tailored for small satellite deployments with a consistent success rate.

- **Photon Spacecraft**: A highly adaptable satellite bus that allows customers to deploy and operate missions without having to build a satellite from scratch.

- **Neutron Rocket (in development)**: A reusable medium-lift rocket designed to compete with SpaceX's Falcon 9 and cater to future human spaceflight and cargo missions.

- **Space Systems Division**: Offers a suite of satellite hardware, including solar panels, star trackers, reaction wheels, and software systems.

- **Mission-as-a-Service**: Provides turnkey mission capabilities that include payload integration, launch, satellite ops, and data services.

Why It's Undervalued

Despite its breakthrough technology and accelerating mission cadence, RKLB remains significantly undervalued by traditional investors. Much of this discount can be attributed to its early-stage status, heavy capital expenditures, and the inherent volatility of the space sector. However, long-term investors with a high tolerance for risk may find current valuations offer an attractive entry point.

Factors contributing to its undervaluation include:

- **Reliable Mission Performance**: A string of successful launches has established Rocket Lab's credibility in an industry where consistency is rare.

- **Defensive Revenue Streams**: Government contracts with agencies such as NASA, the U.S. Space Force, and DARPA add stability to future cash flows.

- **Rapid Vertical Integration**: Acquisitions like Sinclair Interplanetary and Planetary Systems Corporation have added proprietary technologies and talent.

- **Valuable Intellectual Property**: Advanced propulsion systems, unique composite materials, and autonomous flight software set Rocket Lab apart from its peers.

- **Limited Institutional Awareness**: Many institutional investors remain underexposed to the stock, leaving room for future buying pressure.

10x Growth Thesis

Rocket Lab is strategically aligned with multiple megatrends that could fuel exponential growth over the next decade. As global reliance on space-based technologies deepens, Rocket Lab's vertically integrated model and technological edge offer it a unique position to capitalize.

- **Proliferation of Small Satellites**: The demand for cost-effective, reliable launches for Earth observation, communications, and IoT is exploding.

- **Reusable Neutron Rocket**: With a focus on efficiency and sustainability, Neutron could unlock new markets and increase margins.

- **Strong Public Sector Ties**: Contracts from NASA and defense agencies ensure a foundation of recurring and reliable income.

- **Full-Stack Space Services**: Photon enables end-to-end solutions, allowing Rocket Lab to serve both satellite developers and operators.

- **Moon and Deep Space Missions**: Rocket Lab's CAPSTONE mission to the Moon demonstrates its ability to handle complex, high-value missions.

- **Expanding Infrastructure**: Plans for new launch complexes and integration facilities will support higher launch cadence and geographic diversity.

Key Financial Highlights

Rocket Lab is still in its growth phase, and its financials reflect both the challenges and the promise of scaling a capital-intensive business. However, key indicators suggest improving efficiency, growing revenues, and a well-capitalized balance sheet.

- **Revenue Growth**: Generated more than $200 million in 2023, with forecasts suggesting $280–$300 million in 2024 based on mission backlog and new contracts.

- **Contracted Backlog**: Holds over $500 million in contracted revenue, providing visibility into near-term performance.

- **Gross Margin Expansion**: Margins are improving as fixed costs are spread across more frequent missions.

- **Capital Efficiency**: Raised substantial capital through its SPAC merger and has managed to avoid excessive dilution.

- **R&D Investment**: Continues to funnel significant resources into Neutron and space systems to fuel long-term growth.

- **Cash Reserves**: Over $300 million in liquidity ensures runway for development and expansion initiatives.

Risks to Watch

Like any emerging company in a frontier industry, Rocket Lab carries its fair share of risks. Understanding and managing these risks is crucial for investors considering a long position.

- **Execution Risk**: Delays or failures in Neutron's development could impede revenue diversification and growth.

- **Market Volatility**: Capital-intensive models are vulnerable to tightening credit markets and economic downturns.

- **Technical Challenges**: Launch anomalies or payload integration issues could damage client confidence.

- **Competitive Pressure**: Competes with both legacy giants (Boeing, Northrop Grumman) and agile startups (Firefly, Astra).

- **Regulatory Headwinds**: Must navigate international treaties, safety regulations, and geopolitical tensions.

- **Dilution Risk**: Further capital raises could dilute existing shareholders if not paired with meaningful growth.

Analyst Ratings & Insider Sentiment

- **Wall Street Analysts**: Analysts who cover RKLB remain bullish, projecting price targets between $8 and $16 over the next 12 months.

- **Insider Holdings**: CEO Peter Beck and other top executives maintain sizable ownership stakes, aligning their incentives with long-term shareholders.

- **Institutional Positioning**: Institutional interest is slowly building, particularly from innovation-focused and ESG-aligned funds.

Final Verdict

Rocket Lab represents a rare combination of technical excellence, visionary leadership, and strategic positioning within one of the most promising frontiers of the modern economy. As the commercialization of space continues to accelerate, Rocket Lab's full-stack capabilities—from satellite components to orbital delivery—could make it an indispensable partner to both private and public entities.

While the company is not without risks, its innovative approach and expanding footprint offer a highly attractive long-term growth story. If Rocket Lab delivers on its ambitious vision, it has the potential to move from a niche launch provider to a cornerstone of space infrastructure, with returns to match.

RKLB offers investors a front-row seat to the future of space, where the only true limit may be how high the company can fly—and how far its shareholders are willing to ride the journey.

Chapter 8: DLocal Limited – Ticker: DLO

DLocal Limited (NASDAQ: DLO) is a high-growth fintech company operating at the crossroads of two explosive trends: global e-commerce expansion and the digital transformation of emerging markets. As a payment processor tailored specifically for underserved economies, DLocal provides the critical financial rails that enable international merchants to transact seamlessly with billions of consumers in regions traditionally ignored by legacy financial systems. For investors looking to capture value in the rise of digital finance and globalization, DLO represents an innovative, scalable, and globally impactful opportunity with massive long-term upside.

Company Overview

Founded in Montevideo, Uruguay, in 2016, DLocal was created with a mission to simplify and democratize cross-border payments in emerging markets. The founders recognized that global businesses were eager to tap into the spending power of consumers in Latin America, Africa, and Asia, but were blocked by the complexity of fragmented financial systems. DLocal's proprietary payment platform removes these barriers, offering a seamless experience that rivals fintech services in the most developed economies.

DLocal currently operates in more than 40 countries across three continents. Its "One DLocal" platform is built to scale: one API, one contract, and one settlement system allow global companies to operate as if they had a local financial presence in each country. From payment acceptance and disbursements to compliance and fraud prevention, DLocal provides end-to-end financial infrastructure designed for the unique challenges of emerging markets.

Key offerings and strategic advantages:

- **Localized Payment Solutions**: Accepts a wide variety of local payment methods, including mobile wallets, bank transfers, cash-based options, and installment payments.

- **Trusted by Global Giants**: Its clientele includes Amazon, Netflix, Spotify, Meta, Microsoft, and SHEIN, validating its robust infrastructure.

- **Two-Way Payment Flow**: Facilitates both inbound customer payments and outbound mass disbursements for platforms, marketplaces, and app-based services.

- **Regulatory Expertise**: DLocal's on-the-ground teams specialize in navigating complex financial regulations country by country.

- **One-Stop Integration**: Businesses integrate once through DLocal's single API to access dozens of payment systems and compliance protocols worldwide.

Why It's Undervalued

Despite delivering strong financial metrics and securing high-profile clients, DLO has experienced significant stock volatility. Concerns about emerging market exposure, geopolitical instability, and growth sustainability have created a disconnect between DLocal's fundamentals and its market valuation.

Here's why DLocal may be significantly undervalued relative to its intrinsic potential:

- **Sticky Revenue Model**: Transaction-based revenue ensures a high degree of predictability and recurring cash flow.

- **Industry-Leading Margins**: With gross margins north of 70% and EBITDA margins consistently over 30%, DLocal operates at enviable profitability levels.

- **Immense Untapped Markets**: Most countries DLocal serves remain largely cash-dependent. As digital adoption accelerates, payment volumes will rise sharply.

- **Exceptional Client Retention**: High net revenue retention signals not only strong customer satisfaction but expansion within existing accounts.

- **Scalable Infrastructure**: Built as a cloud-native platform, DLocal can expand into new countries or payment types without massive capital outlays.

10x Growth Thesis

DLocal is positioned to capture a massive share of the digital commerce revolution sweeping across the Global South. Its long-term growth story rests on macro trends, technological moat, and its ability to scale alongside e-commerce and app-based platforms worldwide.

- **Trillion-Dollar TAM**: DLocal's total addressable market in cross-border payments for emerging economies exceeds $1 trillion and is growing rapidly.

- **E-Commerce Surge**: Internet and smartphone penetration in emerging markets is catalyzing the digital retail sector, especially among underbanked populations.

- **Digital Financial Inclusion**: DLocal serves populations previously excluded from online commerce, creating first-time access to global goods and services.

- **Geographic Expansion**: The company continues entering new countries annually, diversifying its footprint and reducing reliance on any single market.

- **Client Deepening**: As customers like Amazon and Netflix grow in emerging markets, their transaction volumes processed through DLocal naturally increase.

- **Platform Innovation**: DLocal is investing in AI-driven fraud prevention, real-time reporting tools, and dynamic currency conversion to increase value for clients.

- **M&A Opportunities**: The fragmented nature of fintech in emerging markets gives DLocal multiple opportunities to acquire smaller rivals and consolidate regional dominance.

Key Financial Highlights

DLocal's financial profile showcases a rare combination of profitability, growth, and capital efficiency—particularly impressive for a company still in its early scale-up phase.

- **Revenue Momentum**: DLocal reported over $500 million in TTM revenue as of Q1 2024, growing at more than 30% year-over-year.

- **Sustained Profitability**: Unlike many fintech peers, DLocal has remained profitable every year since going public, even while reinvesting in growth.

- **Robust EBITDA Margins**: Operating margins consistently exceed 30%, indicating strong pricing power and disciplined cost management.

- **Healthy Free Cash Flow**: Generates consistent cash flow, allowing for reinvestment, geographic expansion, and potential shareholder returns.

- **Minimal Leverage**: Maintains a conservative balance sheet with little to no debt, giving it flexibility during macroeconomic downturns.

- **Efficient Capital Allocation**: Low dilution and high return on capital metrics suggest savvy financial stewardship.

Risks to Watch

As with any company operating in dynamic, high-growth environments, DLocal faces meaningful risks:

- **Regulatory Uncertainty**: Diverse jurisdictions mean evolving regulations, requiring continual adaptation and legal oversight.

- **Foreign Exchange Volatility**: Revenue in local currencies and reporting in USD expose DLocal to currency translation risk.

- **Client Concentration**: A small number of major clients contribute a large portion of revenue. Any change in these relationships would be material.

- **Competitive Landscape**: Global payment giants may enter these markets aggressively, increasing pricing pressure.

- **Macroeconomic Fragility**: Inflation, devaluation, and political instability in core markets can reduce consumer spending and transaction volumes.

- **Technology Risk**: As a fintech platform, system outages, fraud, and cybersecurity threats could impact customer trust and revenue.

Analyst Ratings & Insider Sentiment

- **Wall Street Analysts**: Sentiment has improved in recent quarters, with most analysts issuing "Buy" or "Outperform" ratings based on growth trajectory.

- **Institutional Support**: DLocal is gaining momentum among emerging market ETFs and fintech-focused mutual funds.

- **Insider Holdings**: Founders and senior executives continue to hold substantial equity, demonstrating long-term commitment.

- **Recent Insider Activity**: No significant selling pressure, which contrasts with many other tech firms and signals confidence in the growth story.

Final Verdict

DLocal is an under-the-radar gem that addresses one of the most exciting macro opportunities of the next decade: digitizing commerce in emerging markets. The company has developed a technological and regulatory moat that would take years for competitors to replicate. It combines strong fundamentals with powerful tailwinds, positioning it as a long-term winner in global fintech.

For growth-oriented investors with a high risk tolerance and a global perspective, DLO could become a core holding in a portfolio geared toward the future. The company is not only solving a real and pressing problem but doing so with operational excellence and strategic foresight.

As the world becomes more interconnected and inclusive, DLocal's infrastructure could power the financial transformation of billions. Investors who get in early and stay patient may be rewarded handsomely as this story unfolds.

DLO isn't just connecting payments—it's connecting worlds.

Chapter 9: UiPath Inc. – Ticker: PATH

UiPath Inc. (NYSE: PATH) is a trailblazer in the fast-evolving world of robotic process automation (RPA). As businesses race to automate repetitive, time-consuming tasks and embrace large-scale digital transformation, UiPath has emerged as a category-defining platform for building, deploying, and managing software robots. With deep artificial intelligence integration, widespread enterprise adoption, and a massive total addressable market, PATH stands out as a high-potential stock within the AI-driven automation sector. As the digital economy expands, so too does the importance of seamless and intelligent automation—an area where UiPath is primed to lead.

Company Overview

Founded in 2005 in Bucharest, Romania, UiPath has grown from a small Eastern European startup into a global software powerhouse headquartered in New York City. The company specializes in RPA, a form of business process automation technology that allows software bots to mimic human actions across digital systems. These bots can be programmed to perform repetitive tasks such as data entry, invoice processing, onboarding new employees, customer support, and IT system maintenance—freeing up human workers to focus on higher-level strategic initiatives.

UiPath's platform is comprehensive and includes tools for:

- **Process Discovery**: Leveraging AI and analytics to identify workflows ideal for automation.

- **Robot Design & Deployment**: Offering no-code/low-code interfaces so non-technical users can create and test bots quickly.

- **Orchestration**: Managing, scaling, scheduling, and monitoring bots across different systems and departments.

- **AI Integration**: Incorporating technologies like computer vision, machine learning, natural language processing, and GPT-based models to tackle unstructured data and cognitive tasks.

- **Governance & Compliance**: Ensuring automation is secure, traceable, and auditable.

Its customers span nearly every industry, including financial services, healthcare, insurance, telecommunications, logistics, manufacturing, and retail. Notable clients include DHL, PwC, EY, Takeda Pharmaceuticals, NASA, and Autodesk.

Key Differentiators

UiPath is widely recognized for having one of the most comprehensive and scalable end-to-end automation platforms. Key competitive advantages include:

- **User-Friendly Design Studio**: A drag-and-drop interface that democratizes automation development, allowing business users—not just IT teams—to participate.

- **Cloud-Native Flexibility**: Offers deployment options ranging from on-premises to hybrid and full SaaS.

- **Expansive Marketplace**: Hosts thousands of pre-built bots, workflows, and integrations that reduce development time.

- **AI-Enhanced Capabilities**: Through strategic integrations and in-house innovations, UiPath bots can now perform tasks previously reserved for human intelligence.

- **Enterprise-Grade Security & Scalability**: Designed to handle mission-critical workflows at scale, across multinational organizations and industries.

Why It's Undervalued

Despite being a pioneer and dominant player in the RPA industry, UiPath's stock trades well below its IPO highs. This valuation gap presents a compelling opportunity for long-term investors.

Reasons UiPath may be undervalued include:

- **Misunderstood Business Model**: Investors often compare RPA to basic scripts or macros, missing the enterprise-grade capabilities and strategic implications.

- **Temporary Macro Pressures**: IT budget tightening during 2022-2023 created near-term headwinds, but underlying demand for automation is only growing.

- **Exceptional Retention Metrics**: Dollar-based net revenue retention above 120% indicates strong customer loyalty and expansion.

- **Operational Discipline**: A visible path to profitability is now forming, with shrinking operating losses and expanding margins.

- **Strong Balance Sheet**: With over $1.6 billion in cash and no significant debt, UiPath can continue investing aggressively in R&D and strategic acquisitions.

10x Growth Thesis

The future of work is automated, and UiPath is perfectly positioned to lead that charge. Here's why PATH could represent a 10x opportunity in the coming decade:

- **Enormous TAM**: Management estimates the total addressable market for automation solutions exceeds $60 billion, driven by digital transformation across industries.

- **Workforce Augmentation**: As labor shortages and wage inflation persist, companies will increasingly rely on automation to scale operations efficiently.

- **AI + Automation Convergence**: Integrating large language models and generative AI into RPA workflows dramatically increases use cases and functionality.

- **International Growth**: UiPath is expanding into high-growth regions including Asia-Pacific, Latin America, and parts of Europe.

- **Cross-Selling & Platform Expansion**: Customers typically start with automating a single process and then expand adoption across departments, unlocking additional revenue.

- **Robust Partner Network**: Integrations and alliances with companies like Microsoft, SAP, Oracle, and ServiceNow drive distribution and enterprise adoption.

Financial Highlights

UiPath's financials reflect a company balancing rapid growth with a growing emphasis on profitability:

- **Annual Recurring Revenue (ARR)**: Surpassed $1.4 billion as of early 2024, showing reliable, subscription-based income.

- **Revenue Growth**: Continued YoY growth in the 18-25% range, even amidst tough economic cycles.

- **Free Cash Flow**: The business is now generating free cash flow, adding financial flexibility and resilience.

- **Margin Expansion**: Non-GAAP operating margins are improving steadily, with breakeven GAAP profitability in sight.

- **Sticky Revenue Model**: Very low churn rates due to the critical nature of the automation services provided.

Risks to Watch

No investment is without risk. Key factors to monitor include:

- **Intense Competition**: From Microsoft's Power Automate, Automation Anywhere, and emerging AI-first automation startups.

- **Economic Volatility**: Delays in digital transformation budgets during downturns can impact sales.

- **Execution Risk**: Expanding platform functionality while maintaining user-friendliness requires precise execution.

- **Disruptive Technologies**: Rapid AI innovation could render current RPA approaches obsolete if UiPath doesn't adapt quickly.

- **Talent Wars**: As one of the most innovative companies in tech, retaining engineering and sales talent is mission-critical.

Analyst Ratings & Institutional Sentiment

- **Wall Street Analysts**: Generally bullish, with many analysts rating the stock as a "Buy" or "Outperform," especially after consistent earnings beats.

- **Institutional Ownership**: Growing steadily, especially among AI and enterprise software-focused investment funds.

- **Insider Holdings**: Co-founder and former CEO Daniel Dines remains a major shareholder, reinforcing leadership alignment with long-term investors.

Final Verdict

UiPath represents a powerful and underappreciated player in the automation revolution. Its technology solves real-world problems by driving efficiency, reducing operational costs, and freeing up human talent to focus on strategic priorities. With a comprehensive platform, an expanding customer base, growing AI integration, and robust financials, PATH is a serious contender for long-term portfolio growth.

Investors who believe in the convergence of AI, software, and productivity should keep UiPath high on their radar. If execution continues at its current pace and the platform continues to evolve, UiPath could emerge as a defining enterprise software company of the next decade.

Chapter 10: Grab Holdings Limited – Ticker: GRAB

Grab Holdings Limited (NASDAQ: GRAB) is Southeast Asia's leading super-app, providing a vast and growing array of services that range from ride-hailing and food delivery to digital payments and a suite of financial tools. As the region's digital economy surges forward at breakneck speed, Grab stands out as a high-growth tech innovator well-positioned to capitalize on a confluence of transformative trends. These include surging internet adoption, expanding middle-class wealth, smartphone penetration, and an increasingly digital-first consumer base. With active operations across key ASEAN nations such as Singapore, Malaysia, Indonesia, Vietnam, Thailand, and the Philippines, GRAB represents a strategic long-term investment opportunity tied to the digitization of one of the most demographically favorable and economically dynamic regions on the planet.

Company Overview

Launched in 2012 in Malaysia as a modest ride-hailing app, Grab has undergone a remarkable transformation into a multifunctional super-app ecosystem. Now headquartered in Singapore, the company has leveraged its scale, delivery networks, and user engagement to build a one-stop digital platform offering:

- **Mobility**: Comprehensive ride-hailing services that include taxis, private vehicles, motorbike rides, and carpooling options.

- **Deliveries**: Robust capabilities in food, grocery, and e-commerce parcel delivery, supported by logistics innovation.

- **Fintech**: Through GrabPay, the company offers mobile payments, micro-lending, insurance, wealth products, and buy-now-pay-later (BNPL) services.

- **Enterprise**: Includes services for businesses like last-mile logistics, digital advertising, and cloud kitchens tailored for F&B merchants.

Grab's hyperlocal approach ensures tailored offerings that align with cultural nuances, user behavior, and local regulations. The company also enjoys strong brand equity and has formed strategic alliances with major global entities such as Uber (which exchanged its regional business for equity in Grab), Microsoft (providing cloud and AI infrastructure), and Mastercard (collaborating on financial inclusion).

Key Differentiators

Grab differentiates itself through a robust multi-service ecosystem and dominant regional footprint:

- **Integrated Ecosystem**: Users can seamlessly move between services—book rides, order food, shop, pay bills—within a single app, which enhances daily relevance and reduces churn.

- **Hyperlocal Adaptation**: Services are deeply localized—from payment methods to interface language—ensuring high adoption rates.

- **AI & Data Science**: Advanced AI is applied across pricing, routing, safety, personalization, and fraud detection, improving operational excellence.

- **Fintech Expansion**: GrabFin is tapping into Southeast Asia's vast unbanked population, unlocking new revenue streams and financial empowerment.

- **Strategic Collaborations**: Ties with government bodies and tech multinationals facilitate regulatory compliance and product innovation.

Why It's Undervalued

Although Grab is a clear regional leader, investor sentiment has lagged due to macroeconomic volatility and concerns over path to profitability. However, the underlying fundamentals paint a much brighter picture:

- **Profitability Trajectory**: The company is narrowing losses and projecting positive adjusted EBITDA in the near term, aided by growing scale and efficiency.

- **Customer Lock-in**: Super-app usage reduces dependency on paid advertising and enhances monetization across verticals.

- **Macro Tailwinds**: Southeast Asia is undergoing a digital revolution, with rising demand across e-commerce, mobility, and fintech.

- **Room for Expansion**: Penetration remains low in secondary cities and rural markets, offering untapped growth potential.

- **Scalable Model**: Grab's platform is asset-light, relying on partners and network effects to fuel expansion without heavy infrastructure investment.

10x Growth Thesis

Several secular trends and company-specific strategies suggest GRAB has the potential for exponential returns:

- **Favorable Demographics**: The region's young, tech-savvy population is fueling long-term digital adoption and consumption.

- **Fintech Disruption**: As GrabFin scales, it could evolve into a financial super-platform, revolutionizing how millions access credit, savings, and insurance.

- **Tech Advantage**: Proprietary AI tools continuously improve cost structure, user targeting, and service quality.

- **Post-COVID Recovery**: Resumption of travel, tourism, and commuting is catalyzing a rebound in mobility services.

- **Delivery Optimization**: Vertical integration with cloud kitchens and dynamic delivery routing bolsters margins.

- **Government Alignment**: Regional governments are supporting digital infrastructure, financial literacy, and innovation—all areas aligned with Grab's roadmap.

Financial Highlights

Grab is trending toward financial sustainability while maintaining high growth:

- **Revenue Momentum**: Sustained double-digit growth across mobility, deliveries, and financial services.

- **EBITDA Progress**: Year-over-year improvement in unit economics and operational leverage.

- **Liquidity Strength**: Maintains over $4.5 billion in cash and short-term investments, providing flexibility for strategic investments.

- **GMV Leadership**: Exceeds $20 billion annually in gross merchandise value, showcasing ecosystem vitality.

- **User Growth**: Monthly transacting users have risen past 35 million, with increasing ARPU (average revenue per user).

Risks to Watch

Grab's future success hinges on navigating a variety of challenges:

- **Policy Uncertainty**: Local government policies on ride-hailing and fintech may shift, impacting scalability.

- **Market Competition**: Strong rivals like GoTo and emerging local apps create ongoing pricing and market share pressures.

- **Profitability Concerns**: The path to sustained profits is underway but not yet guaranteed.

- **Execution Complexity**: Managing a decentralized business across multiple languages, currencies, and legal systems poses strategic hurdles.

- **FX Volatility**: Exchange rate fluctuations in emerging markets can distort financial reporting and margin expectations.

Analyst Ratings & Institutional Sentiment

- **Wall Street View**: Mixed but improving; several firms have upgraded their outlooks from "Hold" to "Buy."

- **Institutional Backing**: Significant investment by major firms like SoftBank, Altimeter, and other VC-backed tech funds.

- **Insider Holding**: Founders and senior executives retain meaningful equity, signaling long-term confidence in Grab's trajectory.

Final Verdict

Grab Holdings Limited represents one of the most compelling plays in the global digital frontier. As Southeast Asia rapidly transitions into a digital-first economy, GRAB is set to benefit from rising digital adoption, infrastructure expansion, and evolving consumer preferences. With its super-app moat, financial services arm, and improving unit economics, the company is not only surviving in a competitive space—but thriving.

For long-term investors seeking high-growth exposure in the emerging markets of Asia, Grab is an opportunity to ride the next wave of innovation and inclusion. It could easily become one of the defining tech success stories of the decade.

Chapter 11: CleanSpark Inc. – Ticker: CLSK

CleanSpark Inc. (NASDAQ: CLSK) is an innovative Bitcoin mining and energy technology company that has become one of the most talked-about stocks in the crypto-infrastructure sector. With a unique business model that integrates sustainable energy solutions with high-efficiency crypto mining, CleanSpark offers exposure to two megatrends at once: the rise of Bitcoin and the transition to clean, decentralized energy. CLSK is rapidly gaining attention from both retail and institutional investors as a potential long-term winner in the evolving digital asset economy. Its dual focus gives it a competitive advantage, positioning it not only as a key player in the Bitcoin ecosystem but also as a frontrunner in the clean energy revolution.

Company Overview

Founded in 1987 and pivoting to Bitcoin mining in recent years, CleanSpark now operates multiple large-scale mining facilities across the U.S., including in Georgia and Mississippi. Unlike many competitors, CleanSpark takes a differentiated approach by sourcing low-cost, renewable energy to power its mining operations, significantly improving margins and aligning with global ESG trends. The company focuses on:

- **Bitcoin Mining**: Operates one of the largest mining fleets in North America, with over 20 EH/s in projected hashrate and aspirations to expand further.

- **Sustainable Energy Use**: Primarily uses carbon-free energy sources like solar, wind, hydro, and nuclear to power mining rigs around the clock.

- **Grid Services**: Offers microgrid and energy optimization services to external clients, helping balance energy loads and strengthen infrastructure.

- **Strategic M&A**: Acquires distressed or underperforming mining assets and upgrades them for operational efficiency, often at a discount.

This unique combination of vertical integration, technological innovation, and acquisition strategy gives CleanSpark a flexible and resilient operational footprint.

Key Differentiators

CleanSpark stands out from the crowded crypto-mining space in several ways:

- **Energy Arbitrage Strategy**: Utilizes real-time energy pricing to optimize mining profitability, taking advantage of regional rate differences and power market fluctuations.

- **ESG Leadership**: One of the few miners to achieve high renewable usage, making it more palatable for

ESG-focused funds and forward-looking institutions.

- **Vertical Integration**: Controls significant parts of its energy supply and infrastructure, reducing third-party risk and lowering operational costs.

- **Scalable Growth**: Aggressively expanding mining capacity while keeping debt low and maintaining healthy cash reserves, CleanSpark is poised for exponential growth.

- **Tech-Driven Operations**: Implements data-driven analytics and automation in mining operations, allowing for real-time optimization and predictive maintenance.

Why It's Undervalued

Despite massive infrastructure and a top-tier hashrate, CLSK trades at a significant discount compared to peers. Here's why the market may be overlooking its value:

- **Efficient Mining Ops**: Among the most efficient Bitcoin miners, which provides leverage during bull runs and minimizes downside during pullbacks.

- **Bitcoin Exposure**: CLSK provides indirect Bitcoin exposure without the need for a wallet or exchange account, making it ideal for traditional investors.

- **Energy Advantage**: Access to cheaper, greener energy reduces overhead and boosts profitability over time.

- **Market Mispricing**: Shares have lagged despite aggressive expansion and operational upgrades, creating a potential opportunity for value investors.

- **Bitcoin ETF Catalyst**: The rise of Bitcoin ETFs may increase interest in public miners like CLSK as complementary plays.

- **Underrated Balance Sheet**: The company's strong balance sheet is often overlooked but provides flexibility in downturns and expansion opportunities during bull markets.

10x Growth Thesis

CLSK could become a tenbagger in the coming years due to several key catalysts:

- **Bitcoin Halving Cycles**: CLSK's low cost structure allows it to survive and thrive during halving events, when weaker miners get squeezed out.

- **Institutional Rotation**: More hedge funds and pensions are exploring Bitcoin mining stocks for exposure, which could significantly re-rate CLSK's valuation.

- **Energy Innovation**: CleanSpark's focus on sustainable energy aligns with future federal and global climate policy, potentially attracting ESG capital.

- **Hashrate Dominance**: Plans to surpass 50 EH/s could place CLSK among the top global miners, solidifying its competitive position.

- **M&A Pipeline**: Acquiring undervalued assets during bear markets leads to outsized returns in bull markets and enhances long-term scalability.

- **Energy Grid Integration**: Future monetization of its microgrid tech could unlock new revenue streams, further diversifying the business model.

- **Tokenization & Web3**: CleanSpark's energy infrastructure could eventually integrate with Web3 protocols, offering new decentralized applications and partnerships.

Financial Highlights

CleanSpark has shown rapid financial improvement and scalability:

- **Revenue Growth**: Generated over $200 million in revenue in 2023, up significantly YoY, with further increases expected in 2024.

- **Mining Profit Margins**: Maintains industry-leading margins due to low energy costs and highly efficient equipment.

- **Cash Reserves**: Holds over $150 million in cash and crypto assets, enabling flexibility during volatile market conditions.

- **Balance Sheet Strength**: Minimal long-term debt compared to peers gives CleanSpark financial agility.

- **Shareholder-Friendly Moves**: Avoids excessive dilution, focusing on value-added equity raises and responsible capital allocation.

- **Operational Leverage**: With sunk infrastructure costs, CleanSpark stands to benefit disproportionately from rising Bitcoin prices.

Risks to Watch

No investment is without risks. Key issues investors should monitor include:

- **Bitcoin Volatility**: CLSK's revenue is tightly correlated with BTC price movements, and severe downturns can impact profitability.

- **Regulatory Scrutiny**: Potential future restrictions on mining or energy consumption, especially in U.S. states, could introduce headwinds.

- **Weather Events**: Mining facilities may face downtime due to extreme weather in certain regions, disrupting operations.

- **Capital Intensity**: Infrastructure expansion requires significant ongoing investment, and missteps could impact cash flow.

- **Hashrate Arms Race**: Competition from other miners could dilute profitability if BTC prices stall and operational costs rise.

- **Geopolitical Risks**: Global political dynamics may influence energy markets, crypto policy, and supply chain logistics.

Analyst Ratings & Institutional Sentiment

- **Analyst Sentiment**: Generally bullish, with several price targets projecting over 100% upside from current levels.

- **Institutional Activity**: Notable positions held by Vanguard, BlackRock, and other major funds signal increasing legitimacy.

- **Insider Confidence**: Executives continue to buy shares, signaling long-term belief in the business and alignment with shareholders.

- **Retail Buzz**: CLSK remains popular on platforms like Reddit and Twitter, potentially catalyzing short-term momentum during Bitcoin rallies.

Final Verdict

CleanSpark is a top-tier Bitcoin miner that combines sustainability, innovation, and operational excellence. With Bitcoin entering another bull cycle and clean energy gaining traction globally, CLSK is uniquely positioned at the intersection of two disruptive trends. Its efficient, ESG-aligned model makes it not only a viable long-term investment but also a strategic pick for investors seeking exposure to the future of decentralized finance and green technology.

The road may be volatile, but for those with patience and conviction, CLSK offers a compelling asymmetric bet on the digital economy of the future. As more investors realize the hidden value in CLSK's hybrid model, it may become one of the breakout stars of the next crypto cycle.

Chapter 12: TaskUs Inc. – Ticker: TASK

TaskUs Inc. (NASDAQ: TASK) is a digital outsourcing powerhouse that has carved out a highly specialized niche by delivering advanced customer experience (CX) and digital services to some of the world's most innovative and fastest-growing technology companies. In an era when enterprises are actively streamlining operations, scaling digital capabilities, and shifting toward leaner, more agile support systems, TaskUs has positioned itself as a critical partner in the digital transformation journey. The company's hybrid model, combining deeply trained human capital with AI-augmented tools and analytics, makes it a strong and compelling contender in the rapidly evolving outsourced services industry.

Company Overview

Founded in 2008 by two entrepreneurs with a vision to revolutionize business process outsourcing (BPO), TaskUs has transformed from a modest startup into a global leader in digital business services. Over the years, it has built a strong reputation by offering a diverse range of outsourced services such as omnichannel customer support, AI operations, trust and safety, and comprehensive back-office solutions. These services cater to an impressive list of high-growth clients in technology, fintech, e-commerce, health tech, gaming, and social media sectors.

TaskUs currently operates across 26 global delivery sites in key outsourcing hubs including the Philippines, India, Colombia, and Mexico. Its highly optimized and scalable operations model enables it to blend global reach with best-in-class quality. This operational flexibility allows TaskUs to provide tailored solutions that are agile, efficient, and cost-effective.

Core service areas include:

- **Customer Experience (CX)**: 24/7 omnichannel customer support via voice, live chat, email, and social media.

- **Content Security & Trust**: Advanced moderation and trust & safety operations that ensure platforms remain safe and compliant.

- **AI Operations**: High-precision data labeling, annotation, and validation to train AI/ML systems across industries.

- **Back Office Support**: End-to-end services including HR, finance, content operations, analytics, and data processing.

What Makes TASK Stand Out

TaskUs differentiates itself from traditional outsourcing providers through its technology-first culture, innovative service delivery, and deep client integration. Here's what makes it unique:

- **Tech-Enabled Delivery**: The company leverages proprietary AI tools, automation platforms, and real-time analytics dashboards to maximize workforce efficiency and elevate client outcomes.

- **Next-Gen Client Portfolio**: TaskUs serves the who's who of the tech world—hyper-growth unicorns and digital disruptors who require scalability, speed, and sophistication.

- **Scalable Infrastructure**: Its lean, asset-light model enables fast deployment in new geographies and industries, while minimizing capital expenditures.

- **Strong Company Culture**: Recognized repeatedly for its award-winning employee programs, TaskUs focuses on mental health, career growth, and work-life balance—leading to lower attrition and higher quality outputs.

- **Mission-Driven Execution**: The company operates with a values-first mindset, emphasizing people, purpose, and performance, which resonates with modern tech clients.

Why It's Undervalued

Although TaskUs plays a critical role in enabling digital operations for global firms, it remains significantly undervalued relative to its strategic importance and future potential. Here's why:

- **Overcorrected Valuation**: The stock experienced a steep drop after its post-IPO highs in 2021, but the fundamentals remain strong—suggesting a dislocation between price and value.

- **Sticky Revenues & Long-Term Clients**: With deep operational integrations and multi-year contracts, TaskUs enjoys high revenue visibility and minimal client churn.

- **AI Tailwinds**: As more companies build AI products, the need for labeled and curated datasets has exploded. TaskUs provides this "human-in-the-loop" function, which is essential for model accuracy.

- **Operational Efficiency Gains**: The use of automation tools, internal platforms, and analytics has allowed the company to continuously enhance margins, even in competitive environments.

- **Underappreciated Growth Story**: Many investors lump TASK into the traditional BPO category, failing to recognize its differentiated approach, niche dominance, and growth trajectory.

10x Potential Catalyst

Several long-term catalysts could propel TaskUs to 10x its current valuation:

- **AI-Driven Workflows**: The global boom in AI deployment creates long-term demand for human-augmented training, moderation, and data curation—areas where TaskUs thrives.

- **Digital Economy Expansion**: As more startups and digital-native firms scale rapidly, they turn to TaskUs for flexible and reliable operational support.

- **Global Expansion Strategy**: Penetrating new regions such as Eastern Europe and Africa opens up fresh labor pools and client bases.

- **Consolidation Opportunities**: TaskUs is well-positioned to either acquire smaller digital service players or become an attractive acquisition target for larger tech services firms.

- **Cross-Selling Power**: With strong existing relationships, TaskUs can continue to upsell and cross-sell new services and verticals, deepening client penetration.

- **AI Ethics & Moderation Demand**: Increasing government scrutiny of online platforms will boost demand for content moderation and compliance services.

Financial Overview

TaskUs has demonstrated financial resilience and consistent growth, bolstered by a scalable cost structure:

- **Revenue**: Generates over $900 million in annual revenues, with strong double-digit compound annual growth.

- **Gross Margins**: Continuously improving as automation and AI reduce reliance on labor-intensive tasks.

- **Free Cash Flow**: Robust free cash flow generation supports reinvestment, shareholder returns, or M&A.

- **Healthy Balance Sheet**: Low leverage and strong liquidity position TASK for future expansion or defensive resilience.

- **Client Diversification**: Revenue is spread across a wide range of industries and companies, minimizing dependency on any single client.

Risks to Consider

Investors should remain mindful of these potential headwinds:

- **Global Macroeconomic Conditions**: Recession fears or budget tightening could reduce enterprise outsourcing budgets.

- **Wage Inflation**: Salary growth in offshore markets like the Philippines and India may affect cost structures.

- **Content Moderation Scrutiny**: The company's work in content safety could draw public or political controversy.

- **Intensifying Competition**: As BPO and digital outsourcing gain momentum, competition from larger incumbents and AI-first startups could pressure pricing and margins.

- **Client Volatility**: Startups and high-growth clients can be unpredictable, especially during market downturns.

Wall Street Sentiment & Insider Activity

- **Analyst Ratings**: The consensus leans positive, with several analysts maintaining Buy ratings and citing growth potential.

- **Institutional Confidence**: Large asset managers and hedge funds have accumulated TASK shares, reflecting long-term confidence.

- **Insider Commitment**: Founders and key executives hold substantial equity stakes, signaling alignment with shareholder interests.

Final Verdict

TaskUs stands at the intersection of artificial intelligence, digital transformation, and the future of agile business services. Its blend of cutting-edge technology, elite talent, and strategic client partnerships makes it far more than a traditional outsourcing firm. For investors looking for exposure to the back-end infrastructure powering tomorrow's tech giants, TASK represents a high-conviction opportunity. With strong fundamentals, growth catalysts, and an attractive valuation, TaskUs is a potential multi-bagger that deserves a place on every forward-looking investor's radar.

Chapter 13: Oscar Health, Inc. – Ticker: OSCR

Oscar Health, Inc. (NYSE: OSCR) is a next-generation, tech-driven health insurance company aiming to transform the way individuals access, understand, and manage their healthcare. Founded in 2012, Oscar was among the first companies to fully integrate technology, data science, and human-centered design into the health insurance experience. As the broader healthcare sector continues its digital metamorphosis, Oscar Health represents a compelling blend of innovation, disruption, and scalable potential within one of the largest and most complex industries in the United States. With healthcare expenditures exceeding $4 trillion annually, Oscar's mission aligns perfectly with the growing demand for smarter, more accessible, and personalized healthcare services.

Company Overview

Oscar Health was built on a mission to make healthcare simple, transparent, and human. The founders envisioned a system where insurance did not act as a barrier to care but rather as an enabler. The company currently operates in the individual and family ACA markets, small group insurance, and Medicare Advantage, targeting both tech-savvy millennials and historically underserved populations.

Its technology platform sets Oscar apart, offering features like easy appointment scheduling, transparent billing, 24/7 virtual care, and real-time benefit tracking. These functionalities are seamlessly integrated into Oscar's mobile app and web interface, reflecting the company's consumer-first mindset. Oscar's direct-to-consumer distribution model, paired with value-based care partnerships, is revolutionizing how insurers can simultaneously reduce costs and improve health outcomes.

Oscar is now active in over 20 states and continues expanding its national footprint. The company has formed partnerships with major hospital systems and physician groups to strengthen its provider networks, giving members better access to quality care.

Key offerings include:

- **Individual and Family Plans**: ACA-compliant plans designed for affordability, accessibility, and member empowerment.

- **Small Group Plans**: Tailored for businesses with fewer than 50 employees, offering flexible benefit structures and digital-first services.

- **Oscar+ Platform**: A white-label, cloud-based technology platform licensed to other insurers and health systems, unlocking a recurring revenue stream.

- **Virtual Care**: Includes 24/7 telemedicine, remote health monitoring, and digital triage services that reduce healthcare friction and control costs.

What Makes OSCR Stand Out

Oscar Health isn't just another insurance provider; it brings a Silicon Valley ethos to a traditionally risk-averse industry. The company differentiates itself through its relentless focus on user experience, digital innovation, and proactive care:

- **Tech-First Model**: Oscar's app and portal interface are often ranked among the best in the industry, enabling members to manage healthcare as easily as banking or shopping.

- **Data-Driven Personalization**: AI and predictive analytics drive targeted care reminders, preventive screening suggestions, and health insights.

- **In-House Concierge Teams**: Every member is assigned to a dedicated care team, enhancing navigation and satisfaction.

- **Platform-as-a-Service Expansion**: Oscar licenses its technology to third parties, giving it access to scalable SaaS-like margins and reducing reliance on insurance revenue alone.

Oscar's DNA is steeped in digital transformation. Unlike legacy competitors who are digitizing after decades of analog operations, Oscar was digital from day one—allowing greater flexibility, lower operational overhead, and superior adaptability to new healthcare demands.

Why It's Undervalued

Despite its bold vision and tech-forward model, OSCR remains significantly undervalued in public markets for several key reasons:

- **Market Misunderstanding**: Investors often lump Oscar in with high-burn insurtech startups, overlooking its growing efficiency and differentiated strategy.

- **Short-Term Losses**: The company continues to invest heavily in product development and geographic expansion, impacting near-term profitability.

- **ACA Uncertainty**: While concerns persist about the Affordable Care Act's regulatory future, the reality is that ACA participation and bipartisan support have increased.

The result? A stock priced for failure despite growing revenues, improving medical loss ratios, and increasing operational scale.

- **Massive Addressable Market**: U.S. healthcare remains ripe for disruption, and Oscar is well-positioned to capture market share in the trillion-dollar insurance and tech-enabled care space.

- **Scalable Infrastructure**: Oscar+ allows Oscar to scale through third-party adoption without needing to acquire customers directly.

- **Improving Economics**: Key performance indicators such as loss ratios, retention, and customer acquisition costs are all moving in the right direction.

10x Potential Catalyst

Here's how OSCR could deliver tenfold returns over the next 5–10 years:

- **Oscar+ Licensing Revenue**: The company's tech stack could become a foundational platform for other health insurers and providers, bringing in recurring, high-margin revenue.

- **Medicare Advantage Expansion**: A lucrative and fast-growing market with ample room for innovative players to disrupt incumbents.

- **Policy Tailwinds**: Federal and state-level regulations increasingly support virtual care, value-based contracts, and ACA enrollment.

- **AI-Driven Insights**: Oscar's data analytics capabilities could be monetized through partnerships, population health tools, and predictive care platforms.

- **Brand Loyalty & NPS**: Oscar's consumer satisfaction and user-friendly design can drive organic growth through referrals and long-term retention.

Financial Overview

Oscar is making meaningful progress in aligning its operations with long-term profitability:

- **Annual Revenue**: Exceeding $4 billion, with continued top-line growth as membership expands.

- **Medical Loss Ratio (MLR)**: Gradually improving toward industry benchmarks, reflecting better underwriting and smarter care management.

- **Burn Rate and Path to Profitability**: Operating losses are narrowing, and breakeven is projected within the next few years.

- **Cash Reserves**: The company maintains strong liquidity, enabling continued investment in R&D, hiring, and strategic partnerships.

- **Technology ROI**: Every dollar invested in tech infrastructure creates efficiencies that improve margin over time.

Risks to Consider

While Oscar presents strong upside, there are notable risks to monitor:

- **Policy and Regulatory Uncertainty**: Changes in ACA policy or reimbursement models could disrupt Oscar's core business.

- **Execution Risk**: As Oscar grows, managing complexity while preserving its member-first experience will be critical.

- **Competitive Pressure**: Faces entrenched incumbents like UnitedHealth and innovative peers like Clover Health and Devoted.

- **Macroeconomic Environment**: Recession or unemployment spikes may impact ACA enrollment and member acquisition.

- **Tech Scalability**: Platform performance must continue to scale as user volumes grow to maintain satisfaction and avoid outages.

Wall Street Sentiment & Insider Activity

- **Analyst Ratings**: A mix of "Hold" and "Buy" recommendations, with increasing attention following improved quarterly reports.

- **Institutional Holdings**: Oscar is gaining interest from top-tier institutional investors focused on digital health.

- **Insider Confidence**: Founders and senior leadership continue to hold large equity stakes, signaling long-term belief in the company's trajectory.

Final Verdict

Oscar Health is not merely an insurance company—it's a healthcare platform reimagined for the digital age. By blending world-class user experience with scalable technology and data science, OSCR has built the framework to transform the healthcare landscape. With multiple monetization avenues, improving unit economics, and a customer-first philosophy, Oscar stands poised to deliver strong returns for forward-looking investors. Though challenges remain, Oscar Health's long-term vision, innovation stack, and growing adoption make it one of the most exciting under-the-radar growth stories in the healthtech sector today.

Chapter 14: Revolve Group, Inc. – Ticker: RVLV

Revolve Group, Inc. (NYSE: RVLV) is a next-generation fashion retailer that has revolutionized the way apparel is marketed and sold to millennial and Gen Z consumers. Founded in 2003 and headquartered in Los Angeles, the company has become synonymous with trendy, aspirational fashion. Its strong emphasis on influencer marketing, data analytics, and a fully integrated digital platform makes it a unique player in the retail landscape. By understanding the preferences of younger, digitally native shoppers, RVLV has built a powerful brand that is both culturally relevant and financially promising.

Company Overview

What sets Revolve apart from traditional retailers is its agile, technology-driven business model. Through proprietary algorithms and AI-powered consumer insights, the company forecasts fashion trends and manages inventory with precision. This reduces overstock risks and maximizes margins. The brand's curated and frequently updated product mix is further amplified by its vast network of fashion influencers, who promote Revolve's products to millions of followers across Instagram, TikTok, YouTube, and other platforms.

What Makes RVLV Stand Out

- **Influencer Ecosystem**: Revolve pioneered influencer marketing in fashion retail. Its growth is tied closely to a highly curated network of influencers and social media celebrities who drive organic brand awareness, credibility, and conversions. Through events like #RevolveFestival and global influencer trips, RVLV cultivates deep brand loyalty and user engagement.

- **Tech-Enabled Fashion Operations**: The company uses real-time analytics, machine learning, and predictive modeling to fine-tune its product assortment, streamline operations, and dynamically adjust marketing strategies. This enables Revolve to stay ahead of trends and respond quickly to customer demands.

- **Proprietary House Brands**: RVLV owns more than 20 exclusive labels, including L'Academie, Superdown, Lovers + Friends, and more. These brands offer unique styles only available through Revolve, helping to drive higher margins, deepen brand identity, and improve customer retention.

- **Direct-to-Consumer Platform**: With over 95% of sales occurring through its own online platforms, RVLV retains full control over branding, pricing, and customer experience. This allows for deeper engagement and better lifetime value per customer.

Why It's Undervalued

Despite a compelling brand and advanced infrastructure, RVLV's stock has been under pressure due to broader concerns in the retail sector, including inflation, consumer belt-tightening, and inventory cycles. However, this presents a potential opportunity for long-term investors. Key value drivers include:

- **Gen Z and Millennial Tailwinds**: As Gen Z enters peak earning years and Millennials continue to dominate e-commerce spending, RVLV's digital-first, influencer-fueled strategy is well-positioned to capture this demographic's loyalty.

- **Margin Expansion through Vertical Integration**: The growing share of in-house brands and improved supply chain efficiency could enhance gross and operating margins, even amid macroeconomic uncertainty.

- **International Growth Potential**: Currently, the majority of RVLV's business is U.S.-centric, but its international customer base is expanding. A targeted global strategy could unlock substantial new revenue streams in Europe, Asia, and Latin America.

- **Omnichannel Possibilities**: While RVLV is a digital-first brand, it has explored physical retail through pop-up shops and exclusive events. Expanding into curated physical locations could enhance brand awareness and further cement its lifestyle brand image.

10x Potential Catalyst

Revolve could be a long-term multi-bagger if it leverages several growth vectors:

- **Seamless Creator Commerce**: As shopping becomes more embedded within social platforms like Instagram, TikTok, and YouTube, RVLV's close relationship with influencers could translate into immediate, shoppable content with drastically shortened purchase funnels.

- **AI-Powered Personalization and Styling**: By investing in AI technologies that customize product suggestions, emails, and style recommendations, Revolve could significantly improve conversion rates and customer loyalty.

- **Strategic M&A Opportunities**: Acquisitions of smaller niche brands or complementary tech platforms could bolster Revolve's offerings and accelerate growth.

- **Macroeconomic Recovery**: When consumer confidence rebounds, RVLV is well-positioned to ride a new wave of discretionary spending in fashion and lifestyle segments.

Financial Overview

- **Revenue Growth**: RVLV generates over $1 billion in annual revenue, showing robust year-over-year growth pre-COVID and demonstrating resilience during challenging retail environments.

- **Profitability Trends**: While rising logistics and returns costs have squeezed margins in recent quarters, the company remains solidly profitable with a disciplined cost structure and consistent EBITDA generation.

- **Cash Flow and Liquidity**: Revolve maintains a strong balance sheet with substantial cash reserves and positive operating cash flow, allowing for continued investment in technology, marketing, and customer acquisition.

- **Shareholder Returns**: Share repurchase programs signal management's belief in the company's undervaluation and provide incremental upside for long-term shareholders.

Risks to Consider

- **Consumer Spending Volatility**: Fashion is highly cyclical, and economic downturns or reduced discretionary budgets can affect short-term sales.

- **High Return Rates**: E-commerce fashion generally faces high product return rates. While Revolve has implemented systems to mitigate costs, it remains a persistent margin pressure.

- **Saturation of Influencer Marketing**: As influencer marketing becomes more common, its impact may diminish. Revolve must continuously innovate to maintain relevance and effectiveness in this space.

- **Competition from Agile Retailers**: Rivals such as Shein, Zara, and ASOS offer fast fashion at competitive prices, which could erode RVLV's market share unless it continues to differentiate effectively.

Wall Street Sentiment & Insider Activity

- **Analyst Ratings**: Analysts generally rate RVLV as a 'Buy' or 'Outperform,' citing strong digital infrastructure, brand equity, and influencer integration.

- **Executive Ownership**: Founders Michael Mente and Mike Karanikolas maintain significant equity stakes, ensuring alignment with long-term shareholder interests.

- **Institutional Support**: The stock enjoys stable institutional ownership, with prominent investment firms maintaining substantial positions in RVLV.

Final Verdict

Revolve Group is redefining what it means to be a fashion brand in the digital era. By integrating technology, culture, and commerce, RVLV is building a durable competitive moat. Its expertise in trend forecasting, influencer marketing, and e-commerce infrastructure uniquely positions it to scale in a rapidly evolving retail landscape. For growth-oriented investors seeking exposure to fashion, technology, and youth culture, RVLV offers a compelling mix of innovation, resilience, and untapped potential. With the right execution and market conditions, this could be one of the breakout fashion-tech stocks of the next decade.

Chapter 15: Intuitive Machines, Inc. – Ticker: LUNR

Intuitive Machines, Inc. (NASDAQ: LUNR) stands at the cutting edge of the rapidly evolving space exploration industry, focusing primarily on lunar and deep space innovation. Headquartered in Houston, Texas — the heart of America's space program — Intuitive Machines develops advanced technologies and mission-critical services that support NASA's Artemis program, which aims to return humans to the Moon and eventually establish sustainable lunar presence. Beyond government contracts, LUNR is also expanding its footprint into commercial space ventures and partnerships with private space enterprises.

Company Overview

Since its founding in 2013, the company has rapidly built a reputation for solving some of the most complex challenges in space travel, particularly related to precise lunar landings, autonomous surface operations, and reliable in-space communications. Central to its offering is the Nova-C lunar lander, a versatile spacecraft designed to deliver payloads safely and efficiently to the lunar surface. This lander represents one of the most advanced commercial lunar vehicles to date, leveraging proprietary navigation and propulsion technologies developed in-house.

Intuitive Machines' selection by NASA under the Commercial Lunar Payload Services (CLPS) initiative is a testament to its technical prowess and reliability. These awards provide a steady revenue stream while positioning LUNR as a key player in the future of lunar exploration. As global interest in space continues to surge, with countries and private companies alike targeting the Moon and beyond, Intuitive Machines is poised to capitalize on this expanding market.

What Makes LUNR Stand Out

- **Pioneering Lunar Infrastructure**
  Intuitive Machines is a trailblazer in establishing the foundational infrastructure necessary for a sustainable lunar economy. Unlike many competitors who focus solely on launch or satellite technologies, LUNR's comprehensive approach includes payload delivery, surface mobility solutions, and communication networks—key enablers for future lunar bases, mining operations, and scientific research stations.

- **High-Profile Partnerships**
  LUNR's collaborations extend beyond NASA, encompassing partnerships with leading aerospace firms and defense contractors. These alliances not only secure long-term government contracts but also help integrate LUNR's technology into broader space ecosystem projects, diversifying its revenue streams and mitigating risk.

- **Full-Stack Space Technology**
  By controlling a wide segment of the lunar mission value chain—from designing spacecraft and propulsion systems to deploying data relay satellites—LUNR reduces reliance on external vendors and positions itself for multiple revenue avenues. This full-stack capability also allows for greater innovation and faster iteration cycles.

- **Strategic Location**
  Operating near NASA's Johnson Space Center offers critical advantages. The proximity fosters strong communication channels, easier collaboration on R&D, and access to a talent pool with specialized space industry expertise.

Why It's Undervalued

Despite its pioneering status and growing role in the commercial space sector, LUNR remains relatively underappreciated by the broader investment community. Several factors contribute to this undervaluation:

- **Revenue Visibility**
  LUNR's contracts with NASA provide tangible near-term revenue, which differentiates it from speculative space startups still searching for commercial customers. These contracts validate the company's capabilities and reduce financial uncertainty.

- **First-Mover Advantage**
  Being among the first private companies to regularly send payloads to the Moon gives LUNR critical early flight heritage and brand equity. This advantage is invaluable in aerospace, where trust and proven track records dictate future contract awards.

- **Scalable Business Model**
  Each successful mission expands LUNR's operational experience and credibility, unlocking opportunities for repeat contracts and cross-selling additional technologies and services across lunar and orbital missions.

- **Investor Misunderstanding**
  A number of investors continue to perceive space stocks as high-risk speculative plays without appreciating the revenue-generating contracts and long-term structural shifts toward a space-based economy. This disconnect creates a value gap that savvy investors can exploit.

10x Potential Catalyst

LUNR's potential to multiply its value by tenfold depends on a series of scalable developments and market dynamics:

- **Successful Lunar Missions**
  Repeated, flawless mission execution will elevate the company's credibility, making it the go-to contractor for future lunar endeavors. This momentum can drive both contract wins and investor enthusiasm.

- **In-Space Infrastructure**
  LUNR's vision extends beyond one-off landings: it aims to build ongoing lunar communications and navigation networks that provide recurring revenue streams and establish the company as a critical service provider for future lunar bases.

- **Expanding Commercial Demand**
  As commercial activities such as lunar mining, space tourism, and satellite deployment gain traction, the demand for reliable lunar transport and infrastructure will surge, providing new market opportunities for LUNR.

- **International Market Entry**
  By offering delivery services to allied nations and private space agencies worldwide, Intuitive Machines can diversify its customer base and reduce dependency on any single government or commercial client.

Financial Overview

- **Revenue**
  Currently in the early revenue stage, LUNR benefits from NASA contracts and is witnessing increased interest from commercial clients, signaling healthy growth potential.

- **Margins**
  Research and development expenses remain high as the company invests heavily in technology and

mission readiness, which compresses profit margins. However, scale and operational experience are expected to improve margins over time.

- **Cash Flow**
  Intuitive Machines is heavily investing in its infrastructure, including spacecraft development and mission operations, resulting in negative cash flow for now. With successful mission completions and contract expansions, positive cash flow is anticipated in the near to mid-term.

- **Capital Structure**
  Following a recent SPAC merger, the company has bolstered its capital base to fund ongoing missions and technology development. Future capital raises may be necessary as the company scales its operations.

Risks to Consider

- **Execution Risk**
  The complexities and technical challenges of space missions mean that any mission failure could damage LUNR's reputation and negatively affect its stock price.

- **Funding Needs**
  Significant upfront investment is required for spacecraft development and mission execution, which may lead to shareholder dilution or increased debt if additional funding rounds are needed.

- **Competition**
  Major players such as SpaceX, Blue Origin, and emerging startups compete for the same contracts, raising the stakes and potential pressure on pricing and margins.

- **Regulatory and Geopolitical Barriers**
  Space activities are tightly regulated internationally, and geopolitical tensions could impose restrictions or delays on contracts, especially with non-U.S. customers.

Wall Street Sentiment & Insider Activity

- **Analyst Coverage**
  Though still limited, analyst coverage is expanding as mission milestones approach, with experts highlighting LUNR's NASA partnerships and technical innovation.

- **Insider Activity**
  Company founders and executives retain significant equity stakes, signaling strong internal confidence in the company's long-term prospects.

- **Retail Interest**
  LUNR is gaining traction on retail investment platforms, especially following public announcements of successful missions and contract awards, reflecting growing grassroots enthusiasm.

Final Verdict

Intuitive Machines (LUNR) exemplifies a true moonshot investment—both literally and figuratively. With a robust foundation of government contracts, proprietary technology, and a first-mover advantage in commercial lunar logistics, the company offers more than speculative hype. It provides tangible revenue pathways and significant growth potential as humanity's footprint in space expands. For investors with the appetite to withstand volatility and complexity, LUNR presents a unique opportunity to participate in the next frontier of economic growth: the Moon and beyond.

Chapter 16: EyePoint Pharmaceuticals, Inc. – Ticker: EYPT

Company Overview

EyePoint Pharmaceuticals, Inc. (NASDAQ: EYPT) is a specialty biopharmaceutical company focused on developing and commercializing innovative ophthalmic treatments. Headquartered in Watertown, Massachusetts, EyePoint leverages its proprietary sustained-release drug delivery technology to address serious eye diseases, with a particular focus on retinal disorders. By targeting underserved therapeutic areas and utilizing controlled-release systems, the company aims to improve treatment outcomes and reduce the burden of frequent eye injections.

Founded in 1987 and formerly known as pSivida Corp., EyePoint has gone through strategic rebranding and realignment over the years to sharpen its focus on ocular drug delivery. Its Durasert™ platform, a proven miniaturized sustained-release technology, forms the backbone of several of its lead products, giving it a competitive edge in managing chronic eye conditions.

What Makes EYPT Stand Out

- **Proprietary Drug Delivery Platform:** The Durasert™ technology allows for the controlled, long-term release of therapeutic agents directly to the eye. This reduces treatment burden, particularly for conditions requiring frequent intravitreal injections.

- **Clinical Pipeline Strength:** EyePoint's pipeline includes promising candidates like EYP-1901, a sustained-release anti-VEGF treatment for wet age-related macular degeneration (wet AMD), diabetic retinopathy, and retinal vein occlusion. Early trial data has shown favorable safety and efficacy results.

- **Commercial Success with YUTIQ®:** YUTIQ, indicated for chronic non-infectious uveitis, has received FDA approval and is generating growing revenues. It validates EyePoint's drug delivery approach in a real-world setting.

- **Strong Leadership and Partnerships:** The management team has deep experience in ophthalmology and biotech, and EyePoint has established collaborations with industry leaders and research institutions. These alliances help fuel innovation and provide validation of its approach.

Why It's Undervalued

Despite having a commercial product and a promising late-stage pipeline, EYPT remains underappreciated by broader markets:

- **Under-the-Radar Profile:** EyePoint does not receive as much media attention or analyst coverage as larger biotech firms, allowing savvy investors to enter before the crowd.

- **Pipeline Not Fully Priced In:** The value of EYP-1901 and other clinical candidates isn't fully reflected in the stock price, leaving significant room for upward revaluation as milestones are hit.

- **Recurring Revenue Potential:** Unlike traditional eye treatments that require monthly injections, EyePoint's products offer long-term efficacy, potentially leading to recurring sales and high patient adherence.

- **Market Expansion:** With aging populations and rising diabetes prevalence, the addressable market for retinal disease treatments is expanding, giving EyePoint room for organic growth across multiple geographies.

- **Low Market Cap Relative to Potential:** With a market cap still under many of its biotech peers, EYPT trades at a steep discount compared to companies with less advanced technology platforms.

10x Potential Catalysts

EYPT could experience explosive growth due to several high-impact developments:

- **Phase 2/3 Data Readouts:** Positive results from pivotal trials of EYP-1901 in wet AMD or other indications could significantly boost investor confidence and valuation.

- **Regulatory Approvals:** FDA approval of EYP-1901 would open the door to commercial launch and revenue acceleration.

- **Partnerships or Licensing Deals:** Collaborations with larger pharmaceutical companies could bring in non-dilutive capital and enhance distribution capabilities.

- **M&A Potential:** Given its unique platform and late-stage pipeline, EyePoint could become an acquisition target for larger biotech or ophthalmology players.

- **Expansion into Additional Indications:** Leveraging its drug delivery tech for other ocular diseases could broaden its product portfolio and revenue streams.

Financial Overview

- **Revenue:** YUTIQ provides a growing stream of product revenue, although still modest. Future products are expected to scale this significantly as adoption increases.

- **Margins:** Gross margins are healthy, particularly for YUTIQ, with potential improvement as economies of scale kick in.

- **Cash Position:** EyePoint maintains a solid cash runway, especially after recent capital raises, giving it flexibility to fund R&D and commercialization efforts.

- **R&D Spend:** High R&D investment reflects its commitment to advancing the pipeline, especially EYP-1901. This spending is essential to maintain innovation leadership in its niche.

Risks to Consider

- **Clinical Trial Outcomes:** As with all biotech firms, trial failures can significantly impact valuation and future prospects.

- **Regulatory Delays:** Approval timelines are uncertain and subject to extensive FDA review processes, which can push back revenue realization.

- **Competition:** The ophthalmology space includes major players like Regeneron and Roche, who could outpace or challenge EyePoint with their own treatments.

- **Commercial Execution:** Successfully launching and scaling a new therapy requires marketing prowess and physician adoption.

- **Dilution Risk:** As a development-stage biotech, future capital raises could dilute existing shareholders if non-dilutive partnerships aren't secured.

Wall Street Sentiment & Insider Activity

- **Analyst Coverage:** Coverage is increasing, with analysts citing EyePoint's innovative technology and late-stage pipeline as key strengths.

- **Insider Buying:** Executives have shown confidence through recent insider purchases, signaling belief in long-term value.

- **Institutional Interest:** EyePoint has attracted attention from institutional investors seeking high-growth biotech opportunities. Increased ownership from smart money could serve as a vote of confidence.

Final Verdict

EyePoint Pharmaceuticals represents a high-upside opportunity in the biotech space. Its proprietary sustained-release technology, strong pipeline, and existing FDA-approved product position it well for long-term growth. With multiple catalysts on the horizon—including pivotal trial data and regulatory decisions—EYPT could deliver outsized returns for investors willing to navigate the risks inherent in early-stage biotech. For those seeking exposure to the future of ophthalmic innovation, EyePoint offers a compelling, undervalued opportunity with serious 10x potential.

Chapter 17: Opera Limited – Ticker: OPRA

Company Overview

Opera Limited (NASDAQ: OPRA) is a Norway-based technology company best known for its Opera web browser, a unique player in the browser market that has carved out a loyal global user base with its focus on speed, privacy, and innovative features. Originally founded in 1995 and spun off as a standalone entity in 2017, Opera has evolved from a traditional browser provider into a broader platform offering AI integration, fintech services, and e-commerce tools within its ecosystem. With a presence in over 170 countries, Opera reaches hundreds of millions of users, particularly in emerging markets like Southeast Asia, Africa, and parts of Eastern Europe.

Opera distinguishes itself through its lightweight architecture, built-in ad blocker, free VPN service, crypto wallet, and integrated messaging apps, creating a browser experience that resonates with both privacy-conscious and mobile-first users. This commitment to user-centric innovation has enabled Opera to thrive in a space dominated by giants like Google Chrome and Apple Safari.

What Makes OPRA Stand Out

- **Diversified Revenue Streams:** Beyond browser monetization, Opera generates revenue from search partnerships (like with Google and Yandex), fintech services, and advertising, creating a more resilient business model.

- **Focus on Emerging Markets:** Opera's mobile-first strategy targets underserved regions with lighter browsers and features tailored for users with slower internet connections.

- **Built-in Features:** Opera differentiates itself with embedded tools like a free VPN, native crypto wallet, battery saver, and social messaging integrations that enhance user engagement and retention.

- **AI Integration:** Opera has begun incorporating generative AI features directly into its browser, making it more interactive and responsive for tech-savvy users.

Why It's Undervalued

Despite its profitability and expanding ecosystem, OPRA often flies under the radar compared to other tech firms:

- **Low Valuation Multiples:** OPRA trades at modest price-to-earnings and price-to-sales ratios, especially given its high margins and recurring revenues.

- **Consistent Growth:** With strong revenue growth in the past few years, Opera is showing it can expand its user base while maintaining profitability.

- **Overlooked by Analysts:** Opera receives limited analyst coverage relative to its user base and tech developments, creating a potential mispricing opportunity.

- **Cash-Rich Balance Sheet:** The company boasts a strong balance sheet with minimal debt and ample liquidity, giving it flexibility for strategic investments.

10x Potential Catalyst

Opera has several levers that could drive exponential growth:

- **AI-Enhanced Browsing:** Continued rollout of AI-powered tools in the browser could increase user engagement and advertising revenues.

- **Monetization of Fintech Offerings:** In-browser microloans, digital wallets, and payment processing can open lucrative new revenue streams in high-growth markets.

- **User Growth in Underserved Markets:** As internet penetration increases in Africa and Asia, Opera's lightweight browser could capture millions of new users.

- **Strategic Acquisitions or Partnerships:** Opera could expand its ecosystem further by acquiring smaller tech firms or partnering with AI and crypto startups.

Financial Overview

- **Revenue:** Opera has demonstrated strong top-line growth, with quarterly revenues surpassing $90 million in recent periods.

- **Profitability:** The company maintains solid EBITDA margins and continues to generate net income, a rarity among small-cap tech firms.

- **Cash Position:** Opera has a significant cash reserve, providing a buffer against macroeconomic headwinds and the ability to reinvest in R&D.

- **Dividend Policy:** Opera has also issued occasional special dividends, rewarding long-term shareholders while continuing to grow.

Risks to Consider

- **Market Competition:** The browser market is dominated by big players like Google, Apple, and Microsoft, who have far more resources.

- **Ad Revenue Sensitivity:** As with other digital platforms, Opera's advertising revenues are vulnerable to cyclical downturns in global ad spending.

- **Regulatory Risk:** Opera has faced regulatory scrutiny, particularly around lending products in emerging markets, which could affect expansion plans.

- **User Retention Challenges:** While its features are compelling, user loyalty in the browser market is notoriously low and driven by default settings on devices.

Wall Street Sentiment & Insider Activity

- **Analyst Coverage:** Limited, but generally positive, with analysts noting Opera's profitability and innovation as strengths.

- **Insider Holdings:** Founders and key executives hold significant stakes in the company, aligning leadership's interests with shareholders.

- **Retail Attention:** Opera has a quiet but growing following among retail investors who are increasingly aware of its low valuation and tech potential.

Final Verdict

Opera Limited is a hidden gem in the browser and digital services space. Its commitment to innovation, especially in AI and privacy features, sets it apart in a crowded market. The company's diversified revenue model, global user base, and steady profitability give it a solid foundation to capitalize on future digital trends. For investors seeking a tech play with real earnings, scalable potential, and exposure to fast-growing internet markets, OPRA presents a compelling 10x opportunity.

Chapter 18: Symbotic Inc. – Ticker: SYM

Symbotic Inc. (NASDAQ: SYM) is a cutting-edge robotics and automation company that is reshaping the future of warehouse logistics. Headquartered in Wilmington, Massachusetts, Symbotic designs and deploys artificial intelligence-powered robotic systems that automate supply chain operations for some of the largest retailers and wholesalers in the world. The company's core platform integrates AI, robotics, and proprietary software to deliver a more efficient, scalable, and data-rich solution to traditional warehouse operations.

Company Overview

Originally a private company for many years, Symbotic gained significant attention due to its collaboration with Walmart, which helped showcase the potential of its technology on a massive scale. The company went public via a SPAC merger in 2022 and has since continued to win major contracts, including with Target and Albertsons.

Symbotic is tackling one of the most labor-intensive and error-prone sectors—the warehouse and logistics industry—with a unique value proposition: a fully automated system that can process mixed pallets, reduce operational costs, and speed up fulfillment.

What Makes SYM Stand Out

- **Advanced Automation Platform:** Symbotic's system utilizes fleets of autonomous mobile robots, machine vision, and AI-driven software that work in harmony to store, retrieve, and sort goods in real time.

- **Strategic Partnerships:** Walmart, one of the largest retailers in the world, is both a customer and an investor in Symbotic. Their deep integration across Walmart's distribution centers is a testament to SYM's scalability and value.

- **Modular and Scalable:** Unlike some legacy automation systems, Symbotic's solutions are modular. This enables clients to scale operations without overhauling entire facilities.

- **Data-Driven Efficiency:** The system's embedded AI generates valuable insights, enabling predictive inventory management and real-time operational visibility.

- **High Switching Costs:** Once a company integrates Symbotic's platform, switching to a competitor would require massive capital expenditure and operational downtime, creating a sticky customer base.

Why It's Undervalued

Symbotic has already demonstrated strong proof of concept with blue-chip clients, yet it remains undervalued in the broader tech and industrial automation space:

- **Underappreciated Revenue Model:** The company operates under long-term contracts that create recurring revenue streams, which investors often overlook due to its hardware-focused image.

- **Massive TAM (Total Addressable Market):** The global warehouse automation market is expected to surpass $50 billion in the next several years, and Symbotic is well-positioned to capture significant share.

- **Early-Stage Growth Curve:** Symbotic is still in the early innings of expansion, meaning its current valuation may not reflect future cash flow potential.

- **Misunderstood Complexity:** Retail investors may not fully grasp the sophistication and competitive edge of Symbotic's technology, creating an asymmetry of information opportunity.

- **Economies of Scale:** As more systems are deployed, Symbotic benefits from cost reductions and improved margins through manufacturing efficiencies and software improvements.

10x Potential Catalyst

Symbotic's trajectory toward a potential 10x return is driven by a mix of technological excellence, execution, and broader market trends:

- **Expansion with Walmart and Others:** Walmart plans to roll out Symbotic systems across all of its regional distribution centers. As these deployments ramp up, recurring revenues and service fees will grow accordingly.

- **New Client Acquisition:** Beyond Walmart, Symbotic has already landed deals with Target and Albertsons. Expanding to more retail chains, wholesalers, and even e-commerce players like Amazon could fuel exponential growth.

- **Software Monetization:** As Symbotic continues to refine its AI and logistics software, it may begin licensing or providing data analytics services, opening a high-margin revenue stream.

- **Global Expansion:** Most current operations are in North America. Entering international markets could exponentially increase the company's addressable market.

- **Robotics-as-a-Service (RaaS):** Transitioning to a subscription-based or hybrid model could attract more customers while enhancing valuation multiples.

Financial Overview

- **Revenue Growth:** Symbotic has shown triple-digit revenue growth year-over-year, with expectations of continued acceleration as deployments scale.

- **Margins:** Gross margins are improving as the company transitions from early installations to service and software revenue.

- **Backlog:** A significant order backlog provides revenue visibility for the coming years.

- **Cash Position:** The company is well-capitalized post-SPAC merger, but investors should monitor for any future funding needs as growth accelerates.

- **Path to Profitability:** Currently reinvesting heavily in growth, Symbotic is expected to reach profitability within the next few years as more systems go live and service revenue increases.

Risks to Consider

- **Execution Risk:** Managing large-scale deployments and ensuring flawless integration is a complex task that requires operational excellence.

- **Customer Concentration:** Walmart remains its largest customer. Any changes in that relationship could significantly impact revenue.

- **Supply Chain Challenges:** As with any hardware-based business, Symbotic is susceptible to global supply chain disruptions.

- **Technological Displacement:** While Symbotic is currently ahead, rapid advances in robotics and AI from competitors could erode its lead.

Wall Street Sentiment & Insider Activity

- **Analyst Coverage:** Wall Street is beginning to take notice, with several analysts initiating coverage and rating the stock as a high-growth opportunity.

- **Insider Holdings:** Founders and executives maintain significant ownership, aligning their long-term interests with shareholders.

- **Institutional Investment:** Symbotic has attracted investments from respected institutional players, adding credibility to its story.

Final Verdict

Symbotic Inc. is a high-potential growth story sitting at the intersection of AI, robotics, and logistics. The company's proven technology, deep relationships with Fortune 500 clients, and expanding revenue base position it as a long-term winner in warehouse automation. For investors seeking exposure to the future of supply chain technology, SYM offers a compelling blend of innovation, scalability, and asymmetric upside potential. With continued execution and client expansion, Symbotic could very well be a dominant name in logistics tech for decades to come.

Chapter 19: BigBear.ai Holdings, Inc. – Ticker: BBAI

Company Overview

BigBear.ai Holdings, Inc. (NYSE: BBAI) is a cutting-edge technology company that delivers AI-powered decision intelligence solutions for national defense, supply chain optimization, cyber engineering, and more. Headquartered in Columbia, Maryland, BigBear.ai plays a significant role in the transformation of how organizations use data and artificial intelligence to solve complex problems. Originally formed from the merger of multiple advanced analytics and machine learning companies, BigBear.ai has positioned itself as a go-to provider of AI solutions for mission-critical applications.

The company's offerings combine predictive analytics, machine learning, and data curation to provide situational awareness and decision-making insights. BigBear.ai serves both government agencies and commercial clients, with a strong emphasis on the U.S. Department of Defense, intelligence community, and logistics-driven enterprises.

What Makes BBAI Stand Out

- **Government-Grade AI Capabilities:** BBAI provides high-stakes AI services to top-tier government clients, including the U.S. Army and Air Force. These projects enhance the company's credibility and generate recurring revenue through long-term contracts.

- **Commercial Expansion Strategy:** While historically defense-focused, BigBear.ai is actively expanding into commercial verticals such as manufacturing, healthcare, transportation, and finance. This diversification reduces dependency on government spending cycles.

- **Modular AI Platform:** The company's platform is scalable and modular, allowing clients to customize their analytics and AI applications to specific needs. This adaptability is critical for organizations managing large and complex datasets.

- **Strategic Mergers and Acquisitions:** BigBear.ai was created through the merger of several analytics firms, each bringing deep domain expertise. This consolidated approach allows BBAI to offer full-spectrum AI solutions from data ingestion to deployment.

- **Defense-First Validation:** AI tools used in national security applications undergo rigorous vetting.

BBAI's success in these environments demonstrates the robustness and reliability of its solutions.

Why It's Undervalued

BigBear.ai's valuation doesn't yet reflect its long-term growth potential or strategic importance in the growing AI infrastructure space. Here's why BBAI is flying under the radar:

- **Post-SPAC Mispricing:** BBAI went public through a SPAC merger, a route that has led to volatility and investor skepticism. However, the company's fundamentals and long-term contracts provide more stability than its price suggests.

- **High Barrier to Entry:** Few companies can match BBAI's combination of AI sophistication and security clearance. This acts as a moat in defense and intelligence applications.

- **Transition Phase:** As it pivots toward commercial clients, the full financial impact has yet to materialize. Investors focused on current earnings may miss the inflection point coming with commercial revenue growth.

- **Unrecognized Brand:** Unlike AI giants such as Palantir or C3.ai, BBAI lacks mainstream recognition, which limits institutional inflow and analyst attention. That could change rapidly with key wins.

10x Potential Catalyst

BBAI has several potential catalysts that could dramatically re-rate the stock:

- **Commercial Contracts:** Securing large-scale commercial clients in logistics, healthcare, or financial services would validate the company's pivot and diversify its revenue base.

- **Strategic Partnerships:** Teaming up with cloud providers, defense contractors, or logistics firms could exponentially scale distribution and customer acquisition.

- **AI Adoption Tailwinds:** As AI becomes central to digital transformation, BBAI's solutions are poised to be embedded into critical workflows, increasing stickiness and lifetime customer value.

- **Defense Budget Increases:** Continued growth in national defense and cyber intelligence budgets will likely benefit companies like BigBear.ai with proven track records.

- **Improved Investor Sentiment on SPACs:** A market sentiment shift around SPAC-born tech firms could lead to re-evaluation and higher multiples.

Financial Overview

- **Revenue:** BigBear.ai has maintained steady revenue through government contracts, with potential for steep acceleration as commercial deals are signed.

- **Margins:** While margins are compressed due to high R&D and personnel costs, operating leverage should improve as platform reuse increases.

- **Cash Flow:** The company is working toward cash-flow positivity, aided by contract-based revenue and cost controls.

- **Balance Sheet:** BBAI has taken steps to manage debt and maintain liquidity. Strategic capital allocation is essential as the company scales.

Risks to Consider

- **Execution Risk:** Transitioning from a government-focused business to a commercial-heavy model requires sales expertise and marketing investment.

- **Customer Concentration:** A significant portion of revenue still comes from government clients, exposing the company to budget shifts and procurement cycles.

- **Competitive Landscape:** The AI space is increasingly crowded, with giants like Palantir, IBM, and Microsoft investing heavily in similar solutions.

- **SPAC Overhang:** Some investors remain skeptical of SPAC-based companies, limiting short-term price momentum and institutional ownership.

Wall Street Sentiment & Insider Activity

- **Analyst Coverage:** Limited but growing. Some analysts view BBAI as a hidden gem in defense AI, with room for multiple expansion as contracts and results accumulate.

- **Insider Confidence:** Key executives and early investors have shown commitment through equity ownership and long-term strategic vision.

- **Retail Momentum:** BBAI has seen surges in retail interest, especially as AI hype increases and successful government deployments are publicized.

Final Verdict

BigBear.ai is a powerful contender in the AI space with real-world applications, government validation, and expansion opportunities. For investors seeking a lesser-known play on artificial intelligence with asymmetric upside, BBAI presents a compelling case. With a unique mix of defense pedigree and commercial ambition, BigBear.ai could emerge as one of the most valuable AI infrastructure companies of the decade. The company is not without risks, but its technological edge, modular product suite, and focus on mission-critical solutions give it serious 10x potential in the years ahead.

Chapter 20: Ostin Technology Group Co., Ltd. – Ticker: OSTX

Company Overview

Ostin Technology Group Co., Ltd. (NASDAQ: OSTX) is a China-based manufacturer and supplier of display modules, particularly liquid crystal display (LCD) modules, used in a wide range of devices and industries. Founded in 2010 and headquartered in Nanjing, Jiangsu Province, the company provides LCD modules to the consumer electronics, automotive, medical, and industrial sectors. Despite being relatively under the radar in Western investing circles, OSTX is positioning itself to capitalize on global demand for high-quality, customizable display solutions.

The company specializes in the research, development, and manufacturing of display modules that integrate design, quality, and application-specific functionality. It operates multiple production lines and serves both domestic and international clients, leveraging China's robust electronics manufacturing ecosystem.

What Makes OSTX Stand Out

- **Vertical Integration:** Ostin Technology controls much of its production process, from design to manufacturing, giving it greater quality assurance, cost control, and scalability.

- **Diverse Applications:** OSTX's products are used in everything from smartphones and tablets to automotive dashboards, industrial control panels, and even medical diagnostic equipment. This diversification reduces dependency on any one market.

- **Customization Capability:** The company focuses on custom-designed LCD modules, offering solutions tailored to unique client requirements. This positions it favorably compared to competitors offering only standard products.

- **R&D Investment:** Continuous investment in research and development has allowed OSTX to keep pace with evolving technologies such as OLED integration, flexible displays, and touch-screen enhancements.

Why It's Undervalued

Despite its strong industrial footprint and growing global demand for display technologies, OSTX remains underappreciated by the market:

- **Low Market Awareness:** As a Chinese small-cap stock, OSTX does not receive significant media or analyst attention, making it an undiscovered gem for retail and institutional investors alike.

- **Compelling Valuation:** OSTX trades at a low multiple relative to its peers in the electronics manufacturing sector, offering a compelling risk-reward profile for those willing to dive deeper into lesser-known opportunities.

- **Scalable Business Model:** With manufacturing capacity already in place and new product lines under development, Ostin can quickly scale operations as demand increases.

- **Macro Tailwinds:** Global demand for high-quality displays is only growing, especially in the automotive and industrial sectors where display interfaces are becoming increasingly important.

10x Potential Catalyst

OSTX's growth potential hinges on several catalysts that could significantly drive value:

- **Expansion into High-Margin Sectors:** Entry into sectors such as electric vehicles (EVs) and medical diagnostics, where displays require advanced features and command higher margins, can transform the company's revenue profile.

- **International Partnerships:** Collaborations with overseas tech companies could drive export growth and diversify revenue streams beyond China.

- **IPO Proceeds Deployment:** The capital raised during its 2022 U.S. IPO offers the company the financial flexibility to invest in automation, expand R&D, and enhance its global supply chain.

- **Technology Upgrades:** Adoption of next-generation display technologies such as mini-LED and flexible displays could set the company apart from lower-tier competitors.

Financial Overview

- **Revenue:** While still modest by global standards, OSTX has shown revenue resilience and modest growth, supported by its diversified application base.

- **Margins:** As with many manufacturing firms, margins remain under pressure from input costs and competition, but vertical integration helps mitigate some of these effects.

- **Cash Position:** The company has a conservative balance sheet with manageable debt, and IPO proceeds have improved liquidity.

- **CapEx and R&D:** A significant portion of capital is being reinvested into modernizing production facilities and enhancing display technologies, setting the stage for long-term value creation.

Risks to Consider

- **Geopolitical and Regulatory Risk:** As a Chinese-based company listed on a U.S. exchange, OSTX faces regulatory scrutiny and could be impacted by shifting geopolitical dynamics.

- **Supply Chain Vulnerabilities:** Disruptions in raw material supply or logistics bottlenecks can impact production timelines and profitability.

- **Technology Disruption:** The display industry is fast-moving, and failure to adapt to newer display technologies could render OSTX's offerings obsolete.

- **Market Volatility:** As a low-float stock, OSTX can experience heightened volatility, making it more susceptible to sharp price swings.

Wall Street Sentiment & Insider Activity

- **Analyst Coverage:** Coverage is minimal, with few institutional analysts following the stock. This can lead to inefficiencies in pricing and opportunities for early investors.

- **Insider Ownership:** Founders and executives maintain significant ownership stakes, signaling alignment with shareholder interests and long-term commitment.

- **Retail Buzz:** OSTX occasionally garners attention on social media platforms, especially among investors looking for high-risk, high-reward micro-cap plays.

Final Verdict

Ostin Technology Group may not yet be a household name, but its foundational strengths in manufacturing, diversification across industries, and customizable technology offerings make it an attractive speculative investment. While not without risks—especially given geopolitical exposure and market volatility—OSTX presents a unique opportunity to tap into the global demand for advanced display modules. For investors seeking asymmetrical upside in under-the-radar tech hardware plays, OSTX may be worth a closer look.

Chapter 21: Strategy, Portfolio Construction, and Research Habits

Building a high-growth portfolio requires more than picking a few exciting stocks—it demands strategy, discipline, and consistent research. This chapter will guide you through constructing a portfolio using the 20 companies profiled in this book, managing risk, determining position sizes, and staying updated with relevant developments. You'll also learn how to develop habits that help you uncover future 10x opportunities.

How to Build a Portfolio Using These 20 Picks

While each of the 20 companies in this book offers compelling upside potential, it's crucial to diversify across sectors, market capitalizations, and risk levels. Overconcentration in a single theme—such as AI or biotech—can increase volatility and expose you to drawdowns if that sector underperforms.

- **Diversifying by Sector:** The 20 picks include stocks from industries such as AI, biotechnology, space exploration, cybersecurity, e-commerce, and fintech. Aim to group your investments so no single sector makes up more than 20–25% of your portfolio.

- **Diversifying by Market Cap:** A healthy portfolio should balance small-cap disruptors with more stable mid- and large-cap names. Smaller companies like OSTX or LUNR may offer massive upside but come with higher volatility. Offsetting them with firms like SYM or RVLV provides balance.

- **Diversifying by Risk Level:** Some picks are pre-revenue and speculative, while others have commercial products and recurring revenues. Assess the risk-reward profile of each and diversify accordingly.

Suggested Position Sizing and Risk Management

No matter how bullish you are on a particular stock, avoid betting too heavily on any one name. A common rule of thumb is to limit any single position to 5% or less of your total portfolio.

- **Core vs. Satellite Approach:** Consider building a "core" of higher-conviction, less volatile stocks that make up 60–70% of your portfolio. Use the remaining 30–40% for higher-risk, higher-reward plays.

- **Risk Budgeting:** Allocate your capital not just by dollar amount, but by risk exposure. Two $5,000 positions may carry wildly different risks depending on the stock's volatility, financial health, and business model.

Timing: Lump Sum vs. Dollar-Cost Averaging (DCA)

You don't have to invest in all 20 stocks at once. In fact, timing can play a key role in risk management:

- **Lump Sum Investing:** This approach gives you immediate exposure but is best suited for long-term investors who can stomach short-term volatility.

- **Dollar-Cost Averaging:** DCA allows you to spread your entry points over weeks or months. This strategy reduces timing risk and is ideal during volatile market conditions.

Regardless of your method, ensure you revisit your positions regularly and stay disciplined in your allocation strategy.

When to Take Profits or Re-Evaluate

Knowing when to exit is just as important as knowing when to buy.

- **Exit Signals and Red Flags:** Watch for deteriorating fundamentals, loss of key contracts, excessive dilution, or unfavorable regulatory shifts. Significant underperformance vs. peers or broken technical patterns may also warrant action.

- **Long-Term Hold vs. Swing Trade Mindset:** Clarify your time horizon. Some stocks may be "buy and hold" plays based on emerging secular trends, while others may be better suited for swing trades around catalysts. Define your goals upfront.

Set sell targets if you're trading based on a catalyst (e.g., FDA approval or earnings beat). For long-term holdings, consider trimming if a stock becomes overvalued or grows too large relative to your total portfolio.

Keeping Up with Your Picks

Investing is not a "set and forget" endeavor. Staying updated on each of your holdings is critical for timely decisions.

- **How to Track Earnings Reports, News, and Key Events:**

    o   Subscribe to earnings calendars via Yahoo Finance or EarningsWhispers.

    o   Set Google Alerts for each company.

    o   Follow companies on X (formerly Twitter) and LinkedIn.

    o   Use tools like Seeking Alpha to get real-time analysis and updates.

- **Useful Research Tools and Resources:**

    o   **Financial Sites:** Yahoo Finance, MarketWatch, Finviz, and TradingView for charts and fundamentals.

- Newsletters: Consider subscribing to Morning Brew, The Daily Upside, and ARK Invest's newsletters.

- YouTube Channels: Channels like "Everything Money," "Ticker Symbol: YOU," and "Joseph Carlson" offer deep-dive analyses.

- Subreddits: r/stocks, r/investing, and r/pennystocks provide crowd-sourced insight (always do your own research).

- Investor Relations Pages: Always read the company's latest earnings transcripts, 10-Qs, and investor presentations.

Continuing the Journey: How to Find More 10x Opportunities

The companies in this book are just the beginning. To find the next wave of exponential winners, adopt the habits of great researchers:

- **Follow Venture Capital Trends:** See what VCs are funding—many unicorns go public later.

- **Study Secular Megatrends:** AI, automation, decentralized finance, longevity science, and climate tech are examples of long-term themes.

- **Screen for Financial Anomalies:** Use screeners to find high revenue growth, increasing insider buying, or unusual volume spikes.

- **Listen to Earnings Calls:** Go beyond headlines. Hearing management's tone and commentary can reveal confidence—or red flags.

- **Join Investor Communities:** Twitter/X, Discord groups, and newsletters can help surface under-the-radar ideas.

Stay curious, stay disciplined, and above all—never stop learning. The world's next 10x opportunity might be just one insight away.

Conclusion

Investing in high-growth stocks, particularly in innovative sectors like artificial intelligence, biotechnology, and space exploration, offers an unparalleled opportunity to be part of the next wave of technological and economic transformation. These companies often operate on the cutting edge, pushing boundaries that can redefine entire industries. However, it's important to recognize that with such potential for outsized returns comes heightened risk. Markets for these stocks can be volatile, driven by rapid shifts in technology, regulatory changes, or competitive pressures. Patience, discipline, and a clear strategy are essential to weathering the inevitable ups and downs. Remember that high-growth investing is a marathon, not a sprint — the biggest winners often emerge over years, not weeks or months.

Top Lessons from the 20 Picks

Throughout this book, we've explored 20 companies with strong growth trajectories and unique value propositions. Several key takeaways emerge from these picks:

- **Diversification Is Crucial:** The diversity in sectors—ranging from AI software to ophthalmic pharmaceuticals and lunar exploration—illustrates the importance of spreading your investment across different markets. This approach helps reduce sector-specific risks and smooth out overall portfolio volatility.

- **Balance Risk and Reward:** Combining large-cap companies with proven track records alongside smaller, more speculative firms creates a balanced portfolio that can benefit from both stability and explosive growth potential.

- **Understand Your Holdings Deeply:** Each company's success depends on distinct catalysts, whether it's a clinical trial readout, a new technology rollout, or government contract wins. Knowing these drivers helps you make informed decisions about when to add, hold, or exit positions.

- **Timing and Position Sizing Matter:** Whether you choose lump-sum investing or dollar-cost averaging, allocating capital thoughtfully and sizing positions based on risk tolerance and conviction helps protect your portfolio and maximize returns.

- **Stay Adaptable:** The fast pace of innovation means that winners today might face disruption tomorrow. Be ready to reassess your holdings regularly and adjust your portfolio in response to market developments and company fundamentals.

A Recap of the 20 Stocks

1.QBTS	11. CLSK
2.ACMR	12. TASK
3.SOFI	13. OSCR
4.SOUN	14. RVLV
5.NTDOY	15. LUNR
6.BULL	16. EYPT
7.RKLB	17. OPRA
8. DLO	18. SYM
9.PATH	19. BBAI
10.GRAB	20. OSTX

Encouragement to Think Long-Term, Stay Informed, and Keep Researching

The journey of investing in emerging technologies is one of continuous learning and vigilance. Market sentiment can shift rapidly on news, but maintaining a long-term perspective enables you to focus on the fundamental growth drivers that truly matter. Commit to staying informed by following earnings reports, industry news, expert analyses, and broader macroeconomic trends.

The most successful investors don't stop at initial research—they continuously refine their knowledge, track new opportunities, and adapt their strategies. The AI revolution and related high-growth sectors are still in their infancy. Over the next decade, these technologies will reshape economies and lifestyles in profound ways. By cultivating strong research habits and a patient mindset, you position yourself to capture substantial gains from this transformation.

Above all, don't be discouraged by volatility or setbacks. Every investment journey includes challenges, but those who persevere, learn from mistakes, and remain focused on the long-term vision are often rewarded. Use the insights and strategies from this book as a foundation to build your own personalized investment approach, tailored to your goals and risk tolerance.

The future holds immense promise. The 20 companies profiled here represent just the beginning of what's possible. With a diversified portfolio, disciplined strategy, and a commitment to ongoing research, you can confidently navigate the dynamic landscape of high-growth investing and uncover the next 10x opportunity that propels your financial future forward.

Printed in Dunstable, United Kingdom